Unit Resource Guide
Unit 11
Multiplication Patterns

THIRD EDITION

KENDALL/HUNT PUBLISHING COMPANY
4050 Westmark Drive   Dubuque, Iowa   52002

A TIMS® Curriculum
University of Illinois at Chicago

UIC The University of Illinois
at Chicago

The original edition was based on work supported by the National Science Foundation under grant No. MDR 9050226 and the University of Illinois at Chicago. Any opinions, findings, and conclusions or recommendations expressed in this publication are those of the author(s) and do not necessarily reflect the views of the granting agencies.

Printed in the United States of America

1 2 3 4 5 6 7 8 9 10   11 10 09 08 07

Letter Home

Multiplication Patterns

Date: _____

Dear Family Member:

In *Multiplication Patterns,* we return to the study of multiplication and division and we focus on multiplication facts. We also solve word problems involving multiplication and division to help students understand when to use each operation.

In third grade, students become fluent with the basic multiplication facts by developing strategies for learning them. The availability of calculators does not eliminate the need to know the multiplication and division facts. We want students who can quickly estimate answers and perform calculations. For this, a knowledge of the facts is essential.

I put these 6 tiles in 2 rows of 3 tiles, so 6 = 2 × 3.

I wonder whether there are any other ways.

Exploring factors of 6

We will first work with the multiplication facts that involve 0, 1, 2, 3, 5, and 10. We call these the "Handy Facts." Next, we arrange square-inch tiles into rectangles and investigate how multiplication is related to the dimensions of the rectangles. We learn about prime numbers and square numbers. Finally, we look for patterns in the multiplication table.

Help your child by asking what he or she has learned about:

- **Square Numbers.** Ask your child to tell you why the square numbers, 1, 4, 9, 16, and so on, are called "square."
- **Patterns with Nines.** Ask your child to tell you some of the patterns related to the multiplication facts for the nines.
- **Zero.** Take turns making up multiplication and division word problems involving zero.
- **Multiplication Facts.** Students will study multiplication facts in small groups in each unit that follows. For this unit, help your child practice the multiplication facts for the fives and tens using the *Triangle Flash Cards.*

Thank you for taking the time to encourage your child's study of mathematics.

Sincerely,

_____

Carta al hogar

Patrones de la multiplicación

Fecha: _____

Estimado miembro de familia:

En *Patrones de la multiplicación,* regresamos al estudio de la multiplicación y la división y nos concentramos en las tablas de multiplicación. También resolvemos problemas que requieren el uso de la multiplicación y la división para ayudar a los estudiantes a comprender cuándo usar cada operación.

En tercer grado, los estudiantes adquieren dominio de las tablas de multiplicación a través de estrategias para aprenderlas. El uso de calculadoras no elimina la necesidad de saber las tablas de multiplicación y división. Queremos que los estudiantes puedan estimar respuestas y hacer cálculos rápidamente. Para esto, es esencial saber las tablas.

Estudio de los factores del 6

En primer lugar, trabajaremos con las tablas de multiplicación que incluyen los números 0, 1, 2, 3, 5 y 10. Las llamamos "Cómodas tablas de multiplicación". Luego, formamos rectángulos con cuadritos de una pulgada e investigamos de qué manera la multiplicación se relaciona con el tamaño de los rectángulos. Aprendemos acerca de los números primos y los números cuadrados. Por último, buscamos patrones en las tablas de multiplicación.

Ayude a su hijo/a preguntándole qué aprendió acerca de:

- **Números cuadrados.** Pídale a su hijo/a que le explique por qué los números cuadrados 1, 4, 9, 16, etc. se llaman "cuadrados".
- **Patrones con nueve.** Pídale a su hijo/a que le cuente cuáles son algunos de los patrones relacionados con la tabla del nueve.
- **Cero.** Túrnense para inventar problemas de multiplicación y división que usen el cero.
- **Tablas de multiplicación.** En cada una de las próximas unidades, los estudiantes se concentrarán en las tablas de multiplicación en grupos pequeños. En esta unidad, ayude a su hijo/a a estudiar las tablas de multiplicación del cinco y del diez usando las tarjetas triangulares.

Gracias por tomarse el tiempo para animar a su hijo/a en el estudio de las matemáticas.

Atentamente,

Table of Contents

Unit 11
Multiplication Patterns

Unit 11

Outline
Multiplication Patterns

Estimated Class Sessions

10-11

Unit Summary

The study of multiplication and division continues by solving problems about an amusement park called Lizardland. Students also look for patterns in the multiplication table and build rectangular arrays to develop strategies for learning the multiplication facts. They apply these patterns to the multiplication of multiples of 10 and 100. The Adventure Book *Cipher Force!* discusses addition, subtraction, multiplication, and division involving zero. Students learn to use *Triangle Flash Cards* to practice multiplication facts. This unit launches the systematic practice and assessment of the multiplication facts that continues in Units 12–20 in the DPP. The DPP for this unit provides practice with and assesses the multiplication facts for the 5s and 10s.

Major Concept Focus

- multiplication concepts
- division concepts
- multiplication sentences
- division sentences
- division and zero
- *Adventure Book:* zero and the four operations
- multiplication facts strategies
- multiplication facts practice
- multiplication tables
- array model of multiplication
- multiplying by multiples of 10

- turn-around facts
- factors
- square numbers
- prime numbers
- Game: products, factors, and rectangular arrays
- investigating patterns
- money
- communicating problem-solving solutions
- practice and assessment of the multiplication facts for the 5s and 10s

Pacing Suggestions

- In Lesson 4 *Completing the Table,* students assess their fluency with the multiplication facts for the fives and tens and begin a systematic review of those facts they need to study. Work with the remaining groups of facts is distributed throughout the Daily Practice and Problems and Home Practice in each unit. All students should continue learning new concepts and skills while working on the facts.

- Because the math facts program is closely linked to the recommended schedule for teaching lessons, classrooms that differ significantly from the suggested pacing will need to make accommodations to ensure that students receive a consistent program of math facts practice and assessment throughout the year. The *Grade 3 Facts Resource Guide* outlines a study schedule for the math facts for classrooms that move much more slowly through lessons than is recommended in the Lesson Guides. For more information, see the TIMS Tutor: *Math Facts* in the *Teacher Implementation Guide.*

Assessment Indicators

Use the following Assessment Indicators and the *Observational Assessment Record* that follows the Background section in this unit to assess students on key ideas.

A1. Can students represent multiplication and division problems using arrays?

A2. Can students solve multiplication and division problems and explain their reasoning?

A3. Can students multiply numbers with ending zeros?

A4. Can students write number sentences for multiplication and division situations?

A5. Can students use patterns in the multiplication table to develop multiplication strategies?

A6. Can students use turn-around facts (commutativity) to multiply?

A7. Can students solve problems involving money?

A8. Do students demonstrate fluency with the multiplication facts for the 5s and 10s?

Unit Planner

KEY: SG = Student Guide, DAB = Discovery Assignment Book, AB = Adventure Book, URG = Unit Resource Guide, DPP = Daily Practice and Problems, HP = Home Practice (found in Discovery Assignment Book), and TIG = Teacher Implementation Guide.

	Lesson Information	Supplies	Copies/Transparencies
Lesson 1 **Lizardland Problems** URG Pages 26–33 SG Pages 140–144 DPP A–B *Estimated Class Sessions* **1**	**Activity** Students solve multiplication problems by using clues they find in a drawing of the Lizardland Amusement Park. They then write and solve their own multiplication problems about the drawing. **Math Facts** DPP Task B provides practice with multiplication facts. **Homework** Assign the homework on the *Lizardland Problems* Activity Pages. **Assessment** Use the *Observational Assessment Record* to note students' abilities to solve multiplication problems and explain their reasoning.	• 1 calculator per student	• Poster made by enlarging the Lizardland picture found on *Lizardland Problems* SG Pages 140–141, optional • 1 copy of *Observational Assessment Record* URG Pages 13–14 to be used throughout this unit
Lesson 2 **Handy Facts** URG Pages 34–43 DAB Pages 159–164 DPP C–D *Estimated Class Sessions* **1**	**Activity** Students generate the multiplication facts for 0, 1, 2, 3, 5, and 10; record them on a blank multiplication table; and look for patterns among the table entries. **Math Facts** DPP Bit C and Task D provide practice with multiplication facts. **Homework** Assign the *Nickels and Dimes* Homework Pages for homework. **Assessment** Use the *Observational Assessment Record* to note students' abilities to use patterns to learn the multiplication facts.	• counters, number lines, or *100 Charts*, optional	• 1 copy of the *100 Chart* URG Page 41 per student, optional • 1 transparency of *My Multiplication Table* DAB Page 159
Lesson 3 **Multiplication and Rectangles** URG Pages 44–56 SG Pages 145–148 DPP E–H *Estimated Class Sessions* **2**	**Activity** Students arrange square-inch tiles into rectangular arrays. They explore turn-around facts, prime numbers, and squares. They derive multiplication facts and record them on their multiplication tables. **Math Facts** DPP Bit E provides practice with multiplication by 0 and 1. Task F is multiplication fact practice. **Homework** Assign the Tile Problems Homework section on the *Multiplication and Rectangles* Activity Pages. **Assessment** *Questions 3–4* of the Homework section may be used for an assessment.	• 25 square-inch tiles of one color per student	• 2 copies of *Centimeter Grid Paper* URG Page 52 per student • 1 copy of *Three-column Data Table* URG Page 53 per student, optional • 1 copy of *Square-Inch Grid Paper* URG Page 54 per student • 1 copy of *My Multiplication Table* with the 0, 1, 2, 3, 5, and 10 columns completed, DAB Page 159 per student • 1 transparency of *Centimeter Grid Paper* URG Page 52 • 1 transparency of *My Multiplication Table* with the 0, 1, 2, 3, 5, and 10 columns completed, DAB Page 159

	Lesson Information	Supplies	Copies/ Transparencies
Lesson 4 **Completing the Table** URG Pages 57–69 SG Pages 149–151 DAB Pages 165–169 DPP I–L HP Parts 1–2 *Estimated Class Sessions* **2**	**Activity** Students complete their multiplication tables by finding the remaining facts through skip counting or using a calculator. Symmetry in the table is discussed as well as patterns for multiples of nine. Students learn to use the *Triangle Flash Cards* to practice the multiplication facts. **Math Facts** DPP items J and L provide practice with multiplication facts. **Homework** 1. Assign the Homework section of the *Completing the Table* Activity Pages. 2. Students take home their lists of facts they need to study and the *Triangle Flash Cards* to practice the facts with a family member. 3. Assign Parts 1 and 2 of the Home Practice.	• 1 calculator per student, optional • 1 envelope for storing flash cards per student	• 2 *Small Multiplication Tables* (1 for class and 1 for home) URG Page 67 per student, optional • 1 copy of *My Multiplication Table* (completed in Lessons 2 and 3) DAB Page 159 per student • 1 transparency of *My Multiplication Table* (completed in Lessons 2 and 3) DAB Page 159 • 1 transparency of *Multiplication Table* URG Page 66
Lesson 5 **Floor Tiler** URG Pages 70–75 DAB Pages 171–173 DPP M–N *Estimated Class Sessions* **1**	**Game** After spinning two numbers, players use the product to color in rectangles on grid paper. Players take turns spinning and filling in their grids. **Math Facts** DPP Task N provides practice with multiplication facts. **Homework** Students play *Floor Tiler* at home. **Assessment** Use the *Observational Assessment Record* to note students' abilities to represent multiplication using rectangular arrays.	• 1 clear plastic spinner or pencil and paper clip per student pair • 1 crayon or marker per student	• 1 copy of *Centimeter Grid Paper* URG Page 52 per student • 1 transparency of *Centimeter Grid Paper* URG Page 52, optional • 1 transparency of *Spinners 1–4 and 1–10* DAB Page 173, optional
Lesson 6 **Division in Lizardland** URG Pages 76–84 SG Pages 152–154 DPP O–P HP Parts 3–4 *Estimated Class Sessions* **1**	**Activity** Students explore the relationship between multiplication and division through problems about the Lizardland Amusement Park. They discover that there is no turn-around rule for division, and they investigate division involving zero. **Math Facts** DPP items O and P provide practice with multiplication facts. **Homework** 1. Assign the Homework section of the *Division in Lizardland* Activity Pages. 2. Assign Parts 3 and 4 of the Home Practice. **Assessment** Use *Question 17* of the Homework section as an assessment.	• counters, optional	• 1 completed copy of *My Multiplication Table* DAB Page 159 per student • 1 classroom copy of Lizardland poster from Lesson 1, optional

(Continued)

Lesson Information	Supplies	Copies/Transparencies

Lesson 7

Cipher Force!

URG Pages 85–93
AB Pages 77–94

DPP Q–R

Estimated Class Sessions

1

Adventure Book

A group of superheroes and their nine-year-old companion fight crime using addition, subtraction, multiplication, and division with zero.

Math Facts

DPP Bit Q provides practice with multiplication facts using mathhoppers. Task R examines products of 36.

Homework

Remind students to practice at home for the quiz on the multiplication facts using the *Triangle Flash Cards: 5s* and *10s*.

Assessment

1. To assess this lesson, students can write a response to one of the first three Journal Prompts.
2. Use DPP item R to assess students' abilities to write number sentences for multiplication situations.

Lesson 8

Multiples of Tens and Hundreds

URG Pages 94–100
SG Page 155
DAB Page 175

DPP S–T

Estimated Class Sessions

1-2

Activity

Using base-ten pieces, students investigate multiplication by multiples of 10 and 100.

Math Facts

DPP Bit S is the Quiz on 5s and 10s. Task T builds number sense and provides practice with math facts.

Homework

Assign the *Professor Peabody's Multiplication Tables* Homework Page in the *Discovery Assignment Book*.

Assessment

1. Use DPP Bit S and the *Observational Assessment Record* to note students' fluency with the multiplication facts for the fives and tens.
2. Transfer appropriate documentation from the Unit 11 *Observational Assessment Record* to students' *Individual Assessment Record Sheets*.

Supplies (Lesson 8):
- 1 calculator per student
- 1 set of base-ten pieces per student
- overhead base-ten pieces, optional

Copies/Transparencies (Lesson 8):
- 1 completed copy of *My Multiplication Table* DAB Page 159 per student
- 1 transparency of *Professor Peabody's Multiplication Tables* DAB Page 175
- 1 copy of *Individual Assessment Record Sheet* TIG Assessment section per student, previously copied for use throughout the year

Connections

A current list of literature and software connections is available at *www.mathtrailblazers.com*. You can also find information on connections in the *Teacher Implementation Guide* Literature List and Software List sections.

Literature Connections

Suggested Titles

- Calvert, Pam. *Multiplying Menace: The Revenge of Rumpelstiltskin (A Math Adventure).* Charlesbridge Publishing, Watertown, MA, 2006.
- Carroll, Lewis. *Alice's Adventures in Wonderland.* Illustrated by Helen Oxenburg. 1st Candlewick Press Edition. Candlewick Press, Cambridge, MA, 1999. (Lesson 6)
- Hulme, Joy N. *Sea Squares.* Hyperion Books for Children, New York, 1993. (Lesson 3)
- Mills, Claudia. *7 × 9 = Trouble!* Farrar Straus Giroux, New York, 2004.
- Neuschwander, Cindy. *Amanda Bean's Amazing Dream.* Scholastic Press, Inc., New York, 1998.
- Tang, Greg. *The Best of Times: Math Strategies That Multiply.* Scholastic Press, Inc., New York, 2002.

Software Connections

- *Math Arena* is a collection of math activities that reinforces many math concepts.
- *Math Munchers Deluxe* provides practice with basic facts in an arcade-like game.
- *Mighty Math Calculating Crew* poses short answer questions about number operations and money skills.
- *National Library of Virtual Manipulatives* website (http://matti.usu.edu) allows students to work with manipulatives including base-ten pieces, the abacus, and many others.

Teaching All Math Trailblazers Students

Math Trailblazers® lessons are designed for students with a wide range of abilities. The lessons are flexible and do not require significant adaptation for diverse learning styles or academic levels. However, when needed, lessons can be tailored to allow students to engage their abilities to the greatest extent possible while building knowledge and skills.

To assist you in meeting the needs of all students in your classroom, this section contains information about some of the features in the curriculum that allow all students access to mathematics. For additional information, see the Teaching the *Math Trailblazers* Student: Meeting Individual Needs section in the *Teacher Implementation Guide.*

Differentiation Opportunities in this Unit

Games

Use games to promote or extend understanding of math concepts and to practice skills with children who need more practice.

- Lesson 5 *Floor Tiler*

Journal Prompts

Journal prompts provide opportunities for students to explain and reflect on mathematical problems. They can help both students who need practice explaining their ideas and students who benefit from answering higher order questions. Students with various learning styles can express themselves using pictures, words, and sentences. Teachers can alter journal prompts to suit students'

ability levels. The following lessons contain a journal prompt:

- Lesson 2 *Handy Facts*
- Lesson 4 *Completing the Table*
- Lesson 7 *Cipher Force!*
- Lesson 8 *Multiples of Tens and Hundreds*

Extensions

Use extensions to enrich lessons. Many extensions provide opportunities to further involve or challenge students of all abilities. Take a moment to review the extensions prior to beginning this unit. Some extensions may require additional preparation and planning. The following lessons contain extensions:

- Lesson 3 *Multiplication and Rectangles*
- Lesson 5 *Floor Tiler*

Unit 11

Background
Multiplication Patterns

In this unit—the third of four multiplication and division units in the third grade—we focus on multiplication facts. Students engage in activities that will help them develop strategies for learning the facts. We expect students to have a variety of strategies for dealing with the facts in third grade and to achieve fluency by the end of the year. This unit introduces the array model of multiplication, investigates multiplication and division with zero, and explores the patterns found when multiplying by multiples of 10 and 100.

Facts

While an understanding of concepts is our highest priority, the existence of calculators does not eliminate the need to know the multiplication and division facts. "However, calculators do not replace fluency with basic number combinations, conceptual understanding, or the ability to formulate and use efficient and accurate methods for computing." (National Council of Teachers of Mathematics, p. 145) For this, a knowledge of the facts is essential. *Math Trailblazers* takes a more conceptual approach to the learning of the basic facts and computation in general. Research has shown that fact retention is higher when facts are learned in a meaningful way. As children investigate patterns among the multiplication facts and use them in problem-solving situations and games, they will develop the ability to quickly recall them when needed.

"Fluency with the basic number combinations develops from well-understood meanings for the four operations and from a focus on thinking strategies." (National Council of Teachers of Mathematics, p. 152) Fluency with basic procedures enhances conceptual understanding of new material.

Practice

Practice is an essential part of developing fluency with the basic facts. In this unit, students are

introduced to the *Triangle Flash Cards* to practice their multiplication facts. These same cards will be used in fourth grade to practice division facts. By using these cards to practice the basic facts, students strengthen their understanding of multiplicative reasoning, e.g., the relationships between factors and multiples and between multiplication and division.

Arrays

In previous units, children worked with multiplication as a way to solve problems about equal groupings and jumps on the number line. In this unit, they will use arrays to represent multiplication.

An **array** is an arrangement of elements into a rectangular pattern of (horizontal) **rows** and (vertical) **columns.** For example, a candy box that contains 5 rows with 6 pieces in each row is a 5 × 6 array. One virtue of the array model is that it makes very clear that 5 × 6 = 6 × 5: The box can be rotated 90 degrees to form a 6 × 5 array. Another advantage is that it creates a visual image of a multiplication problem.

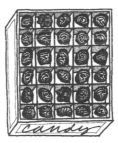

Figure 1: *From left to right, a 5 × 6 array and a 6 × 5 array*

Rate Problems

Problems involving rates occur often in the real world. Although many adults remember memorizing formulas to solve rate problems (for example, "distance = rate × time"), rate problems can be as simple as these:

- If there are 12 eggs in a dozen, how many eggs are there in three dozen?
- If we have 6 pencils in one package, how many do we have in five packages?
- If we travel 60 miles per hour, how far will we travel in 3 hours?

In the first example, the rate is the number of eggs per dozen (12); in the second example, it is the number of pencils in one package (6); and in the third, the rate is the distance we travel in 1 hour (60 miles). Students worked with a rate (8 lemons per pitcher) in the activity *Lemonade Stand* in Unit 7.

Rate problems play an important role in many of the labs in Grades 3–5. In many of these labs, students will determine the appropriate rate from a graph.

Division Involving Zero

While multiplication involving a zero factor always results in zero as the product (any number times zero is zero), there are two different cases of division involving zero.

1. Zero as a dividend. When zero is divided by any (non-zero) number, the answer is zero. For example, suppose a mother distributes all the cookies in the cookie jar equally among her three children. If there are six cookies, each child will get $6 \div 3 = 2$ cookies. Similarly, if there are zero cookies, each child will get $0 \div 3$ cookies. Children will unhappily see that $0 \div 3 = 0$.

2. Zero as a divisor. Division by zero is undefined. Here are a few ways to see why division by zero does not make sense:

   a. Division is the inverse of multiplication. Thus, to solve a problem like $45 \div 9 = N$, we ask, "What number times 9 equals 45?" Since $5 \times 9 = 45$, we know that $45 \div 9 = 5$. Similarly, to solve the problem $45 \div 0$, we would ask, "What number times 0 equals 45?" There is no such number, so it is impossible to divide 45 by zero. If we had the same discussion for another number, we would come to the same conclusion, as long as that number is itself not equal to 0. In paragraph c, we will discuss why $0 \div 0$ is not defined.

   b. Division can also be viewed as repeated subtraction. A simple way to divide by a whole number is to repeatedly subtract

that number from the dividend until zero is reached; the quotient is the number of times the divisor is subtracted. For example, to solve $15 \div 5 = N$, we can proceed as follows:

$$
\begin{array}{r}
15 \\
- 5 \\
\hline
10 \\
- 5 \\
\hline
5 \\
- 5 \\
\hline
0
\end{array}
$$

Since 5 was subtracted three times, we know there are three fives in 15 so that $15 \div 5 = 3$. Now, try the same thing when 0 is the divisor, as in $15 \div 0 = N$:

$$
\begin{array}{r}
15 \\
- 0 \\
\hline
15 \\
- 0 \\
\hline
15 \\
- 0 \\
\hline
15
\end{array}
$$

It is clear that no progress is being made. If we try to divide by zero by subtracting repeatedly until nothing is left, we will be at it forever. Hence, division by zero is not possible. An example of this can be found in the Adventure Book *Cipher Force!* The silly superhero, Div, tries to fill a roller coaster with 24 Girl Scouts by putting zero scouts in the first car, zero scouts in the second car, and so on until all 24 Girl Scouts are on the roller coaster. Even an infinitely long roller coaster would not fill the bill!

   c. It is tempting to believe that $0 \div 0 = 1$. After all, $7 \div 7 = 1$, $5 \div 5 = 1$, so we could decide that $0 \div 0 = 1$. Using the definition of division in terms of multiplication, $0 \div 0 = N$ means $0 = 0 \times N$. While $N = 1$ does make this number sentence true, so would any other number. Since there is not a unique number that satisfies the condition, $0 \div 0$ is undefined.

There are other ways to see why division by zero does not make sense. All of them require examining the meaning of division.

Resources

- National Research Council. "Developing Proficiency with Whole Numbers." In *Adding It Up: Helping Children Learn Mathematics.* J. Kilpatrick, J. Swafford, and B. Findell, eds. National Academy Press, Washington, DC, 2001.

- National Research Council. "Teaching for Mathematical Proficiency." In *Adding It Up: Helping Children Learn Mathematics.* J. Kilpatrick, J. Swafford, and B. Findell, eds. National Academy Press, Washington, DC, 2001.

- *Principles and Standards for School Mathematics.* National Council of Teachers of Mathematics. Reston, VA, 2000.

Observational Assessment Record

A1 Can students represent multiplication and division problems using arrays?

A2 Can students solve multiplication and division problems and explain their reasoning?

A3 Can students multiply numbers with ending zeros?

A4 Can students write number sentences for multiplication and division situations?

A5 Can students use patterns in the multiplication table to develop multiplication strategies?

A6 Can students use turn-around facts (commutativity) to multiply?

A7 Can students solve problems involving money?

A8 Do students demonstrate fluency with the multiplication facts for the 5s and 10s?

A9 _____

Name	A1	A2	A3	A4	A5	A6	A7	A8	A9	Comments
1.										
2.										
3.										
4.										
5.										
6.										
7.										
8.										
9.										
10.										
11.										
12.										

Name	A1	A2	A3	A4	A5	A6	A7	A8	A9	Comments
13.										
14.										
15.										
16.										
17.										
18.										
19.										
20.										
21.										
22.										
23.										
24.										
25.										
26.										
27.										
28.										
29.										
30.										
31.										
32.										

Daily Practice and Problems
Multiplication Patterns

A DPP Menu for Unit 11

Two Daily Practice and Problems (DPP) items are included for each class session listed in the Unit Outline. A scope and sequence chart for the DPP is in the *Teacher Implementation Guide*.

Icons in the Teacher Notes column designate the subject matter of each DPP item. The first item in each class session is always a Bit and the second is either a Task or Challenge. Each item falls into one or more of the categories listed below. A menu of the DPP items for Unit 11 follows.

Ⓝ **Number Sense** C, D, F, H, I, L, Q, R, T	✖ **Computation** A, E, H, I, T	🕐 **Time** G, M	🖳 **Geometry** N
Math Facts B–F, J, L, N–T	$ **Money** J–L, P	🔢 **Measurement**	📈 **Data**

Practicing and Assessing the Multiplication Facts

By the end of third grade, students are expected to demonstrate fluency with the multiplication facts. In Units 3–10, students explore multiplication patterns and develop strategies for learning the multiplication facts. In this unit, they begin the systematic, strategies-based practice and assessment of these facts. This study will take place primarily in the Daily Practice and Problems and will continue through Unit 20. The multiplication facts will be studied and assessed in groups. The sequence in which the groups will be reviewed and studied is shown in Figure 2.

Unit	Multiplication Facts
11	Practice and assess the 5s and 10s
12	Practice and assess the 2s and 3s
13	Practice and assess the square numbers
14	Practice and assess the 9s
15	Practice and assess the last six facts
16	Practice and assess the 2s, 5s, and 10s
17	Practice and assess the 3s and 9s
18	Practice and assess the square numbers
19	Practice and assess the last six facts
20	Assess all the multiplication facts groups

Figure 2: *Distribution of the multiplication facts in Units 11–20.*

Lesson 4 introduces the use of the *Triangle Flash Cards: 5s* and *10s* for studying the multiplication facts. Flash cards for each remaining group are distributed in Units 12–15 in the *Discovery Assignment Book,* immediately following the Home Practice. See the DPP menu above for items that provide practice with multiplication facts. Bit S is a quiz on fives and tens.

For information on studying the facts in Grade 3, see the Daily Practice and Problems Guide for Unit 3. For a detailed explanation of our approach to learning and assessing the math facts in Grade 3, see the *Grade 3 Facts Resource Guide* and for information for Grades K–5, see the TIMS Tutor: *Math Facts* in the *Teacher Implementation Guide.*

 **Daily Practice and Problems**

Students may solve the items individually, in groups, or as a class. The items may also be assigned for homework. The DPPs are also available on the Teacher Resource CD.

Student Questions	Teacher Notes

A **Mental Arithmetic: Adding 99**

Write down these problems; then, solve them. Look for patterns.

1. 131 + 99 =   2. 555 + 99 =

3. 97 + 99 =   4. 103 + 99 =

5. 355 + 99 =   6. 769 + 99 =

7. 327 + 99 =   8. 82 + 99 =

9. 777 + 99 =

TIMS Bit

Discuss possible strategies for finding the answers to these problems. One strategy is to add 100 and subtract 1.

1. 230   2. 654
3. 196   4. 202
5. 454   6. 868
7. 426   8. 181
9. 876

B **Multiplication Story**

1. Write a story and draw a picture about 3 × 5. Write a number sentence on your picture.

2. Write a story and draw a picture about 9 × 5. Write a number sentence for your picture.

TIMS Task

1. 3 × 5 = 15
2. 9 × 5 = 45

Students may wish to share their stories with the class.

Discuss students' pictures. Ask students if they can use their pictures to solve 3 × 15.

C Fives and Tens

A. $5 \times 2 =$

B. $10 \times 2 =$

C. $5 \times 4 =$

D. $10 \times 4 =$

E. $5 \times 6 =$

F. $10 \times 6 =$

G. $5 \times 8 =$

H. $10 \times 8 =$

I. $5 \times 10 =$

J. $10 \times 10 =$

What patterns do you see?

TIMS Bit

A. 10	B. 20
C. 20	D. 40
E. 30	F. 60
G. 40	H. 80
I. 50	J. 100

Students may see that 10 times a number is twice 5 times that number (because 10 is twice 5). They may also see that solutions in the first column skip count by tens and solutions in the second column skip count by twenty.

D Guess My Number

1. I am less than 3×4. I am greater than 2×3. I am an even number. I am not 10.

2. I am less than 4×5. I am greater than 2×7. I am 3 times some number. I am not 15.

TIMS Task

1. 8
2. 18

Student Questions	Teacher Notes

E Multiplication Facts: 0s and 1s

A. $5 \times 0 =$ B. $5 \times 1 =$

C. $10 \times 0 =$ D. $1 \times 10 =$

E. $0 \times 47 =$ F. $47 \times 1 =$

G. $0 \times 736 =$ H. $1 \times 736 =$

I. Use your calculator to check your answers.

J. What can you say about multiplying numbers by 0?

K. What can you say about multiplying numbers by 1?

TIMS Bit

After students complete these questions discuss them with the class.

A. 0   B. 5

C. 0   D. 10

E. 0   F. 47

G. 0   H. 736

J. Numbers multiplied by 0 equal 0.

K. Numbers multiplied by 1 equal themselves.

F More Fives and Tens

A. $5 \times 3 =$ B. $10 \times 3 =$

C. $5 \times 5 =$ D. $10 \times 5 =$

E. $5 \times 7 =$ F. $10 \times 7 =$

G. $5 \times 9 =$ H. $10 \times 9 =$

What patterns do you see?

TIMS Task

A. 15   B. 30

C. 25   D. 50

E. 35   F. 70

G. 45   H. 90

Refer to the Teacher Notes for Bit C.

G Counting by Fives

1. Count by 5-minute periods from 1:00 to 2:00. Make a list.

2. How many 5-minute periods are there from 1:00 to 2:00?

3. How many 5-minute periods are there in two hours?

TIMS Bit

Skip counting may help prepare students to solve problems involving elapsed time. Such problems will appear in Unit 14 Lesson 1.

1. Starting with 1:00, 1:05, 1:10, 1:15, etc.

2. 12

3. 24

Student Questions	Teacher Notes

 Story Solving

Write a story and draw a picture about $5 \times \frac{1}{4}$. Write a number sentence for your picture.

TIMS Task

$5 \times \frac{1}{4} = 1\frac{1}{4}$. Students may wish to share their stories with the class.

 Lizardland Picnic

At Lizardland, eight people can sit at a table in Picnic Park. If your class had a picnic there (including your teacher), how many tables would you need? Draw a picture to show your answer.

TIMS Bit

Answers will vary according to class size.

 Nickels and Dimes

You may use real or pretend money to help you solve the following problems.

1. What is the total value of 6 nickels and 4 dimes?

2. A. The total value of 55¢ is made up of 2 dimes and how many nickels?

   B. Name three other ways you can make 55¢ using only nickels and dimes.

TIMS Task

1. 70¢

2. A. 7 nickels

   B. Students should list at least 3 of the following five other ways:

   5 dimes and 1 nickel

   4 dimes and 3 nickels

   3 dimes and 5 nickels

   1 dime and 9 nickels

   0 dimes and 11 nickels

Cookies

At Max and Cora's cookie stand, one cookie costs 35¢. How many different ways can you pay exact change for one cookie using only nickels, dimes, and quarters?

TIMS Bit

There are 6 possibilities. A table may help students organize their work.

5¢	10¢	25¢
0	1	1
2	0	1
1	3	0
3	2	0
5	1	0
7	0	0

 More Nickels and Dimes

True or false? Explain how you know.

1. 4 dimes < 6 nickels

2. 7 dimes and 4 nickels = 9 dimes

3. 15 nickels > 6 dimes

TIMS Task

Have real or pretend money available to help students solve the problems.

1. False; 4 dimes is 40 cents, 6 nickels is 30 cents.

2. True; the 4 nickels can be exchanged for 2 dimes.

3. True; $.75 is greater than $.60.

M **Missing Time**

Copy each list below. Find the missing times.

1. 2:50, 2:55, ____, 3:05, ____, ____, 3:20

2. 4:15, 4:30, ____, ____, 5:15, ____, 5:45

3. 6:00, 5:55, ____, 5:45, ____, ____, 5:30, ____

4. 8:30, ____, 7:30, ____, 6:30, 6:00, ____

TIMS Bit

You may choose to work with a clock, showing the position of the hands for each of the times given in the problems.

Here are the missing times:

1. 3:00, 3:10, 3:15

2. 4:45, 5:00, 5:30

3. 5:50, 5:40, 5:35, 5:25

4. 8:00, 7:00, 5:30

Multiplication and Rectangles

A rectangle is made from 3 rows with 8 tiles in each row.

1. Draw this rectangle on *Centimeter Grid Paper*.

2. How many tiles make up the rectangle? Write a number sentence to show your answer.

3. Make a different rectangle with the same number of tiles. How many rows? How many tiles in each row?

TIMS Task

1.

2. 3 × 8 = 24 tiles

3. Answers will vary.

   Possible responses:
   1 row of 24 tiles;
   2 rows of 12 tiles;
   4 rows of 6 tiles;
   6 rows of 4 tiles;
   8 rows of 3 tiles;
   12 rows of 2 tiles;
   24 rows of 1 tile

 Lizardland

Use the picture of Lizardland in the *Student Guide* to help you solve the following problems.

Find the Lizardland wall at the entrance to the park.

1. How many bricks are behind the Lizardland sign? Tell how you know.

2. How many bricks are covered by the sign listing the admission prices? Tell how you know.

TIMS Bit

1. 5 × 6 = 30 bricks
2. 6 × 4 = 24 bricks

Student Questions	Teacher Notes

P How Much and How Many?

TIMS Task

A. Moe spent 9 nickels and 7 dimes to buy ice cream. How much money did he spend? Show how you found your answer.

A. $1.15;

    9×5 cents $= 45$ cents

    7×10 cents $= 70$ cents

    45 cents $+$ 70 cents $= 115$ cents

B. Joe has 5 shirts. Each shirt has 3 pockets. How many pockets are on Joe's shirts? Write a number sentence.

B. $3 \times 5 = 15$ pockets

C. $7 \times 5 = 35$ beads

C. Flo has 7 braids in her hair. Each braid has 5 beads. How many beads are in Flo's hair? Write a number sentence.

Q Mathhoppers

TIMS Bit

1. A +3 mathhopper starts at 0 and hops six times. Where does it land?

1. 18

2. 40

2. A +5 mathhopper starts at 0 and hops eight times. Where does it land?

3. No, a +5 mathhopper lands only on numbers ending in 0 or 5. It will land on 160 and then 165. It will jump right over the sunflower seed.

3. A +5 mathhopper starts at 0 and wants to eat a sunflower seed on 163. Will it be able to land on the sunflower seed? Why or why not? Think about the patterns you found in your multiplication table.

Student Questions	Teacher Notes

 R   **A Product of 36**

Write 36 as a product of two numbers in as many ways as you can.

TIMS Task

Have tiles and graph paper available so students can work with arrays to find the answers.

1×36 2×18 3×12

4×9 6×6

S   **Quiz on 5s and 10s**

A. $5 \times 2 =$ B. $3 \times 10 =$

C. $5 \times 0 =$ D. $8 \times 10 =$

E. $6 \times 10 =$ F. $5 \times 3 =$

G. $10 \times 9 =$ H. $7 \times 5 =$

I. $10 \times 2 =$ J. $10 \times 7 =$

K. $6 \times 5 =$ L. $5 \times 10 =$

M. $8 \times 5 =$ N. $9 \times 5 =$

O. $4 \times 10 =$ P. $4 \times 5 =$

Q. $10 \times 10 =$ R. $5 \times 5 =$

TIMS Bit

This quiz is on the first group of multiplication facts, the 5s and 10s.

We recommend 2 minutes for this test. Allow students to change pens after the time is up and complete the remaining problems in a different color.

After students take the test, have them update their *Multiplication Facts I Know* charts.

Student Questions	**Teacher Notes**

 Mathhopper

You may use a calculator to solve the problems. A +8 mathhopper starts at 0.

1. There is a frog at 97. Will the mathhopper land on the frog and be eaten? Tell how you know. If it does not land on the frog, how close does it get?

2. How many hops does the mathhopper need to take to get to a daisy at 224? Tell how you know.

TIMS Task

1. Discuss the patterns of the multiples of 8. Since they are even, it will not land on 97. It lands on 96; one away from the frog. If your calculator has the constant feature press: 8 + 8 = = = = etc. Each time you press =, the constant number (8) and operation (addition) are repeated.

2. 28 hops.

   With the constant feature press: 8 + 8 = = = = etc. Count the number of times you press the equal sign.

   Help students recognize that division can be used. Using the calculator, press: 224 ÷ 8 =.

   Alternatively, 10 hops gets the mathhopper to 80, 20 hops to 160, 30 hops to 240. That's too far. Two hops back is 224, so the answer is 28 hops.

   Other strategies that may be used are repeated subtraction and trial and error.

Lizardland Problems

Lesson Overview

Students solve problems involving multiplication by using clues they find in a drawing of the Lizardland Amusement Park. They write and solve their own multiplication problems about the drawing.

Key Content

- Solving and writing problems involving multiplication.
- Communicating solutions and strategies verbally and in writing

Math Facts

DPP Task B provides practice with multiplication facts.

Homework

Assign the homework on the *Lizardland Problems* Activity Pages.

Assessment

Use the *Observational Assessment Record* to note students' abilities to solve multiplication problems and explain their reasoning.

Curriculum Sequence

Before This Unit

Students developed multiplication concepts by solving word problems in Grade 3 Unit 3 and Unit 7.

After This Unit

Students will continue to develop multiplication concepts through problem solving in Grade 3 Unit 16 Lesson 2 *Fill 'er Up,* Unit 19 *Multiplication and Division Problems,* and the Daily Practice and Problems.

Materials List

Supplies and Copies

Student	Teacher
Supplies for Each Student • calculator	**Supplies**
Copies	**Copies/Transparencies** • poster made by enlarging the Lizardland picture found on *Lizardland Problems*, optional (*Student Guide* Pages 140–141) • 1 copy of *Observational Assessment Record* to be used throughout this unit (*Unit Resource Guide* Pages 13–14)

All blackline masters including assessment, transparency, and DPP masters are also on the Teacher Resource CD.

Student Books
Lizardland Problems (*Student Guide* Pages 140–144)

Daily Practice and Problems and Home Practice
DPP items A–B (*Unit Resource Guide* Page 17)

Note: Classrooms whose pacing differs significantly from the suggested pacing of the units should use the Math Facts Calendar in Section 4 of the *Facts Resource Guide* to ensure students receive the complete math facts program.

Assessment Tools
Observational Assessment Record (*Unit Resource Guide* Pages 13–14)

Daily Practice and Problems

Suggestions for using the DPPs are on page 30.

A. Bit: Mental Arithmetic: Adding 99

(URG p. 17)

Write down these problems; then, solve them. Look for patterns.

1. 131 + 99 =
2. 555 + 99 =
3. 97 + 99 =
4. 103 + 99 =
5. 355 + 99 =
6. 769 + 99 =
7. 327 + 99 =
8. 82 + 99 =
9. 777 + 99 =

B. Task: Multiplication Story

(URG p. 17)

1. Write a story and draw a picture about 3 × 5. Write a number sentence on your picture.
2. Write a story and draw a picture about 9 × 5. Write a number sentence for your picture.

Before the Activity

You may wish to hang the Lizardland poster in the classroom a few days before the activity begins. Ask students to begin thinking of math questions they could ask about the poster.

Teaching the Activity

Ask students to solve *Questions 1–5* on the *Lizardland Problems* Activity Pages. They will have to look carefully at the picture (on the wall or in their books) to find the information needed to answer the problems. Students can solve all the problems using multiplication; however, they should be allowed to use any methods they wish, including calculators. Encourage students to check their answers by finding solutions in different ways.

It is important for students to talk about their solution strategies. For this reason, we recommend they work together in pairs. A whole-class discussion should follow to allow students to talk about different solution paths. Highlight the ways multiplication is used in the problems and include appropriate number sentences. Emphasize the relationship between addition number sentences and multiplication sentences.

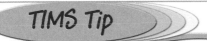

Ask students to trade and solve each other's Lizardland problems.

Question 5 asks students to write their own multiplication problems. Students enjoy working with larger numbers, so their problems might involve numbers that they do not yet know how to multiply. Do not discourage students from using large numbers; problems that are too hard can be modeled with base-ten pieces or solved using calculators. Problems involving two-digit by one-digit multiplication will be dealt with in Unit 19, but many students will enjoy thinking about them now.

Student Guide - page 140

Student Guide - page 141

To solve these problems, look for clues in the picture of Lizardland on the previous pages. Write about how you solved each problem. Use number sentences, pictures, or words.

1. Mr. Brown bought ice cream for his five children at the stand near Picnic Park. How much did he spend?

2. How many blocks are in the wall? Include the blocks that are covered by signs.

3. Each block in the front wall is 8 inches high.
   A. How high is the wall?
   B. Could you climb over it?
   C. Could you jump over it?
   D. Explain.

4. George has been watching the Lizard-Go-Round. It takes 30 seconds to go around one time.
   A. How many minutes does it take to go around eight times?
   B. How many times does it go around in $2\frac{1}{2}$ minutes?

5. Write a problem about Lizardland, and solve it using multiplication.

Homework

Refreshments

1. Tom is at the refreshment stand with his parents. They are buying three hot dogs, two fries, two lemonades, and one milk. How much will their order cost?

Student Guide - page 142 *(Answers on p. 32)*

Math Facts

For DPP Task B students write a story and draw a picture for 9×5 and 3×5.

Homework and Practice

- Nine problems are provided for homework on the *Lizardland Problems* Activity Pages in the *Student Guide*.

- Select a few of the problems students wrote during the activity to assign for homework as well.

- Using DPP Bit A students build mental math skills by adding 99 to three-digit numbers.

Assessment

Use the *Observational Assessment Record* to note students' progress solving multiplication problems and explaining solution strategies.

Buying Balloons

2. Mary's mother bought one balloon for Mary and one for Louise. How much did she pay?

3. José is near the Lizard Kingdom. How much did his balloons cost?

The Skyway

4. Joel wants to ride the Skyway. He is the one in line who is wearing the big hat and sunglasses. He noticed that a new car is loaded every 2 minutes. How long will he have to wait after the car that is now being loaded leaves?

The Lizard Show

5. Seats for today's Lizard Show are selling fast. So far, $400 has been collected. How many seats are left? Show your work with number sentences.

Student Guide - page 143 *(Answers on p. 32)*

Leaping Lizard Roller Coaster

6. How many people can ride in all eight cars of the roller coaster at one time?

7. Jean wants to ride the roller coaster. There are 24 people in front of Jean. She is the one at the end of the line. Will there be enough room for her the next time it is loaded, or will she have to wait?

Ticket Sales

8. The Moore family—Grandmother Moore, Mr. and Mrs. Moore, and the three Moore children—is eating lunch beside Lizard Lake. It is Saturday. How much did they spend on admission tickets for the carnival? (Hint: The admission ticket price is beside the ticket taker at the front gate.)

9. How much would the Moores have saved on admission if they had come on Tuesday?

Student Guide - page 144 *(Answers on p. 33)*

Math Facts and Daily Practice and Problems

DPP Bit A builds math skills and number sense. Task B provides practice with multiplication facts.

Teaching the Activity

1. Display the picture of the Lizardland Amusement Park on the *Lizardland Problems* Activity Pages in the *Student Guide*.
2. Students complete *Questions 1–5.*
3. Discuss the strategies used and the solutions found for each problem.

Homework

Assign the homework on the *Lizardland Problems* Activity Pages.

Assessment

Use the *Observational Assessment Record* to note students' abilities to solve multiplication problems and explain their reasoning.

Answer Key is on pages 32–33.

Notes:

To solve these problems, look for clues in the picture of Lizardland on the previous pages. Write about how you solved each problem. Use number sentences, pictures, or words.

1. Mr. Brown bought ice cream for his five children at the stand near Picnic Park. How much did he spend?

2. How many blocks are in the wall? Include the blocks that are covered by signs.

3. Each block in the front wall is 8 inches high.
   A. How high is the wall?
   B. Could you climb over it?
   C. Could you jump over it?
   D. Explain.

4. George has been watching the Lizard-Go-Round. It takes 30 seconds to go around one time.
   A. How many minutes does it take to go around eight times?
   B. How many times does it go around in $2\frac{1}{2}$ minutes?

5. Write a problem about Lizardland, and solve it using multiplication.

Refreshments

1. Tom is at the refreshment stand with his parents. They are buying three hot dogs, two fries, two lemonades, and one milk. How much will their order cost?

142   SG • Grade 3 • Unit 11 • Lesson 1   Lizardland Problems

Student Guide - page 142

Buying Balloons

2. Mary's mother bought one balloon for Mary and one for Louise. How much did she pay?

3. José is near the Lizard Kingdom. How much did his balloons cost?

The Skyway

4. Joel wants to ride the Skyway. He is the one in line who is wearing the big hat and sunglasses. He noticed that a new car is loaded every 2 minutes. How long will he have to wait after the car that is now being loaded leaves?

The Lizard Show

5. Seats for today's Lizard Show are selling fast. So far, $400 has been collected. How many seats are left? Show your work with number sentences.

Lizardland Problems   SG • Grade 3 • Unit 11 • Lesson 1   143

Student Guide - page 143

*Answers and/or discussion are included in the Lesson Guide.

Student Guide (pp. 142–143)

1. $2.50

2. 150 blocks or 160 blocks; the actual wall has 15 columns of blocks. However, to allow for the space in the margins, the wall was divided. One of the columns of blocks was cut down the middle. If students do not realize this they may count 160 blocks. Accept either answer if it is properly explained.

3. A. 80 inches
   B. Possibly
   C. No
   D. 80 in is almost 7 ft tall (12 in × 84 in)

4. A. 4 minutes
   B. 5 times

5. Answers will vary.* Two possible problems are: How much would it cost for 3 hamburgers and 3 milks? ($2.00 × 3) + (75¢ × 3) = $8.25

   The 2 P.M. Lizard Show sold out. If everyone leaving the show bought an ice cream bar, how much would the ice cream vendor collect? 300 × 50¢ = $150.00

Homework

1. $9.25

2. $1.50

3. $4.00 (José has six balloons and 3 balloons cost $2.)

4. 8 minutes

5. 100 seats are left; $400 ÷ $2.00 = 200 seats; 300 seats − 200 seats = 100 seats

Student Guide (p. 144)

6. 32 people

7. Yes, there will be enough room for Jean.

8. $27.00; children: $9.00; adults: $18.00

9. Save $9.00; on Tuesday, the total would be
$18.00; children: $4.50; adults: $13.50
Alternatively, you save $1.50 for each person
and $6 \times \$1.50 = \$9.00$.

Leaping Lizard Roller Coaster

6. How many people can ride in all eight cars
of the roller coaster at one time?

7. Jean wants to ride the roller coaster. There
are 24 people in front of Jean. She is the one
at the end of the line. Will there be enough
room for her the next time it is loaded, or will
she have to wait?

Ticket Sales

8. The Moore family—Grandmother Moore, Mr. and Mrs. Moore, and the
three Moore children—is eating lunch beside Lizard Lake. It is
Saturday. How much did they spend on admission tickets for the
carnival? (Hint: The admission ticket price is beside the ticket taker at
the front gate.)

9. How much would the Moores have saved on admission if they had
come on Tuesday?

144   SG • Grade 3 • Unit 11 • Lesson 1   Lizardland Problems

Student Guide - page 144

Lesson 2

Handy Facts

Lesson Overview

Estimated Class Sessions

1

Students generate the multiplication facts for 0, 1, 2, 3, 5, and 10; record them on a blank multiplication table; and look for patterns in the table entries. The homework problems use nickels and dimes as a natural setting for practicing the facts for 5 and 10.

Key Content

- Using a multiplication table to record and retrieve multiplication facts.
- Identifying and using patterns among the multiplication facts for 0, 1, 2, 3, 5, and 10.
- Solving problems involving nickels and dimes.

Key Vocabulary

- factor
- multiple
- product

Math Facts

DPP Bit C and Task D provide practice with multiplication facts.

Homework

Assign the *Nickels and Dimes* Homework Pages for homework.

Assessment

Use the *Observational Assessment Record* to note students' abilities to use patterns to learn the multiplication facts.

Materials List

Supplies and Copies

Student	Teacher
Supplies for Each Student • counters, number lines, or *100 Charts,* optional	**Supplies**

Copies
 	
• 1 copy of the *100 Chart* per student, optional
  (*Unit Resource Guide* Page 41)
	Copies/Transparencies
	
	• 1 transparency of *My Multiplication Table*
	  (*Discovery Assignment Book* Page 159)

All blackline masters including assessment, transparency, and DPP masters are also on the Teacher Resource CD.

Student Books

My Multiplication Table (*Discovery Assignment Book* Page 159)
Practicing Handy Facts (*Discovery Assignment Book* Page 161)
Nickels and Dimes (*Discovery Assignment Book* Pages 163–164)

Daily Practice and Problems and Home Practice

DPP items C–D (*Unit Resource Guide* Page 18)

Note: Classrooms whose pacing differs significantly from the suggested pacing of the units should use the Math Facts Calendar in Section 4 of the *Facts Resource Guide* to ensure students receive the complete math facts program.

Assessment Tools

Observational Assessment Record (*Unit Resource Guide* Pages 13–14)

C. Bit: Fives and Tens (URG p. 18)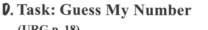

A. $5 \times 2 =$ B. $10 \times 2 =$

C. $5 \times 4 =$ D. $10 \times 4 =$

E. $5 \times 6 =$ F. $10 \times 6 =$

G. $5 \times 8 =$ H. $10 \times 8 =$

I. $5 \times 10 =$ J. $10 \times 10 =$

What patterns do you see?

D. Task: Guess My Number
(URG p. 18)

1. I am less than 3×4. I am greater than 2×3. I am an even number. I am not 10.

2. I am less than 4×5. I am greater than 2×7. I am 3 times some number. I am not 15.

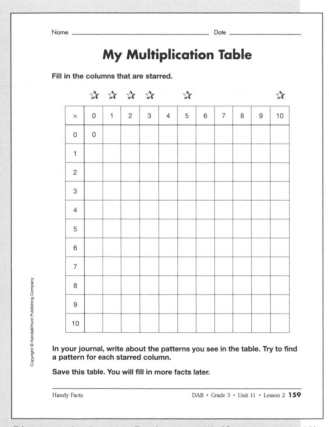

Name _____ Date _____

My Multiplication Table

Fill in the columns that are starred.

☆ ☆ ☆ ☆   ☆   ☆

×	0	1	2	3	4	5	6	7	8	9	10
0	0										
1											
2											
3											
4											
5											
6											
7											
8											
9											
10											

In your journal, write about the patterns you see in the table. Try to find a pattern for each starred column.

Save this table. You will fill in more facts later.

Handy Facts   DAB • Grade 3 • Unit 11 • Lesson 2 **159**

Discovery Assignment Book - page 159 *(Answers on p. 42)*

Teaching the Activity

Tell students they will fill in the columns under the starred numbers (0, 1, 2, 3, 5, 10) on the *My Multiplication Table* Activity Page in the *Discovery Assignment Book*. These columns were chosen because these multiplication facts are easy to remember and are frequently familiar to children.

Students benefit from using concrete ways to figure out their multiplication facts. Encourage them to use one of the following methods.

1. arranging counters or tally marks into groups

2. skip counting orally or on a *100 Chart,* number line (as a mathhopper would), or calculator

TIMS Tip

Be sure students save their tables since they will need them to record more facts throughout the unit.

Begin by filling in the column under 2 together, demonstrating where the products should be written on the transparency of the *My Multiplication Table* Activity Page. Then, ask students to fill in the columns under 1, 3, 5, and 10.

The 0 column deserves a special discussion. To help students understand the zero facts, tell them two types of stories:

> For problems such as 7 × 0: *I have 7 pockets. Each pocket contains 0 pennies. How many pennies do I have in my pockets?*
>
> For problems such as 0 × 7: *The queen had several boxes that each contained 7 diamonds. She gave me 0 of the boxes. How many of the diamonds did she give me?*

Students will enjoy making up and sharing some stories of their own about zero. Afterwards, ask them to fill in the 0 column and the 0 row of their tables.

As students fill in each column, ask them to describe any patterns they find. You may need to rephrase their descriptions of the patterns to help clarify their ideas. Use the terms **factor, product,** and **multiple** where appropriate. Tell them that many people use patterns to remember the facts, as seen in Figure 3.

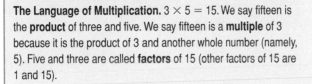

Content Note

The Language of Multiplication. 3 × 5 = 15. We say fifteen is the **product** of three and five. We say fifteen is a **multiple** of 3 because it is the product of 3 and another whole number (namely, 5). Five and three are called **factors** of 15 (other factors of 15 are 1 and 15).

×	0	1 ☆	2 ☆	3 ☆	4	5 ☆	6	7	8	9	10 ☆
0	0	0	0	0	0	0	0	0	0	0	0
1	0	1	2	3		5					10
2	0	2	4	6		10					20
3	0	3	6	9		15					30
4	0	4	8	12		20					40
5	0	5	10	15		25					50
6	0	6	12	18		30					60
7	0	7	14	21		35					70
8	0	8	16	24		40					80
9	0	9	18	27		45					90
10	0	10	20	30		50					100

Figure 3: *The multiplication table as filled in during this activity*

Name _____ Date _____

Practicing Handy Facts

Solve the following problems. Use your multiplication table when you need help.

1. $3 \times 2 =$ _____   2. $6 \times 10 =$ _____   3. $0 \times 10 =$ _____

4. $6 \times 5 =$ _____   5. $8 \times 10 =$ _____   6. $7 \times 1 =$ _____

7. $4 \times 1 =$ _____   8. $9 \times 3 =$ _____   9. $6 \times 2 =$ _____

10. $1 \times 4 =$ _____   11. $9 \times 5 =$ _____   12. $5 \times 5 =$ _____

13. 7   14. 7   15. 8   16. 3
    $\times 5$ $\times 2$ $\times 5$ $\times 3$

17. 3   18. 6   19. 0   20. 1
    $\times 5$ $\times 0$ $\times 2$ $\times 3$

21. 4   22. 2   23. 2   24. 5
    $\times 5$ $\times 3$ $\times 5$ $\times 2$

Write and solve a multiplication story about zero. Write a number sentence to go with it.

_____

_____

_____

_____

_____

Handy Facts   DAB • Grade 3 • Unit 11 • Lesson 2 **161**

Discovery Assignment Book - page 161 *(Answers on p. 42)*

Journal Prompt ✏️

Describe a pattern you find in the multiplication table. Explain why you think this pattern occurs.

PATTERNS FOR REMEMBERING THE FACTS

Patterns for 0 • All multiples of 0 are 0.

Patterns for 1 • Any number times 1 is itself.

Patterns for 2 • All multiples of 2 are even.

• All multiples of 2 are doubles.

• All multiples of 2 end in 0, 2, 4, 6, or 8.

Patterns for 5 • All multiples of 5 end in 0 or 5. When even numbers are multiplied by 5, the product ends in 0. When odd numbers are multiplied by 5, the product ends in 5.

Patterns for 10 • All multiples of 10 end in 0.

• When ten is multiplied by any number, the product is the same number with an extra 0 on the end.

Students might also observe that they get the same answer when they change the order of the factors. For example, $10 \times 3 = 3 \times 10$. This will be more apparent later when they work with a completed multiplication table.

The *Practicing Handy Facts* Activity Page in the *Discovery Assignment Book* provides practice using the table and in remembering the facts for 0, 1, 2, 3, 5, and 10. Have students complete it after they have discussed their patterns.

Math Facts

Task D provides practice with multiplication facts through number puzzles. DPP Bit C provides practice with the multiplication facts for the 5s and 10s.

Homework and Practice

The *Nickels and Dimes* Homework Pages provide practice with the multiplication facts for the fives and tens using money.

Assessment

Use the *Observational Assessment Record* to note students' abilities to use patterns to learn the multiplication facts.

Name _____ Date _____

Nickels and Dimes
Homework

1. Complete the following table by counting money (real or pretend) or by using arithmetic.

Number of Nickels	Number of Dimes	Value of Nickels	Value of Dimes	Total Value
5	3	$.25	$.30	$.55
7	2			
	4	$.40		
	8	$.30		
2			$.90	
4			$1.00	
3			$.30	$.45
		$.05	$.50	
0	7			
9			$.10	$.55

Handy Facts   DAB • Grade 3 • Unit 11 • Lesson 2 **163**

Discovery Assignment Book - page 163 *(Answers on p. 43)*

Name _____ Date _____

2. How many ways can you make $.45 using only nickels and dimes? List them in the table below.

Number of Nickels	Number of Dimes	Value of Nickels	Value of Dimes	Total Value

164 DAB • Grade 3 • Unit 11 • Lesson 2   Handy Facts

Discovery Assignment Book - page 164 *(Answers on p. 43)*

At a Glance

Math Facts and Daily Practice and Problems

DPP Bit C and Task D provide practice with multiplication facts.

Teaching the Activity

1. Use a transparency of the *My Multiplication Table* Activity Page in the *Discovery Assignment Book* to fill in the column under 2 as a class.
2. Students fill in the columns under 1, 3, 5, and 10 using counters, tally marks, or skip counting.
3. Discuss multiplication by zero, by telling two types of stories that involve zero. Ask students to create and share similar stories and then fill in the column under 0.
4. Students discuss patterns they see in the table.
5. Students complete the *Practicing Handy Facts* Activity Page using the multiplication table.

Homework

Assign the *Nickels and Dimes* Homework Pages for homework.

Assessment

Use the *Observational Assessment Record* to note students' abilities to use patterns to learn the multiplication facts.

Answer Key is on pages 42–43.

Notes:

100 Chart

1	2	3	4	5	6	7	8	9	10
11	12	13	14	15	16	17	18	19	20
21	22	23	24	25	26	27	28	29	30
31	32	33	34	35	36	37	38	39	40
41	42	43	44	45	46	47	48	49	50
51	52	53	54	55	56	57	58	59	60
61	62	63	64	65	66	67	68	69	70
71	72	73	74	75	76	77	78	79	80
81	82	83	84	85	86	87	88	89	90
91	92	93	94	95	96	97	98	99	100

Name _____ Date _____

My Multiplication Table

Fill in the columns that are starred.

☆ ☆ ☆ ☆   ☆   ☆

×	0	1	2	3	4	5	6	7	8	9	10
0	0										
1											
2											
3											
4											
5											
6											
7											
8											
9											
10											

In your journal, write about the patterns you see in the table. Try to find a pattern for each starred column.

Save this table. You will fill in more facts later.

Handy Facts   DAB • Grade 3 • Unit 11 • Lesson 2 **159**

Discovery Assignment Book - page 159

Discovery Assignment Book (p. 159)

My Multiplication Table

×	0	1	2	3		5					10
0	0	0	0	0		0					0
1	0	1	2	3		5					10
2	0	2	4	6		10					20
3	0	3	6	9		15					30
4	0	4	8	12		20					40
5	0	5	10	15		25					50
6	0	6	12	18		30					60
7	0	7	14	21		35					70
8	0	8	16	24		40					80
9	0	9	18	27		45					90
10	0	10	20	30		50					100

Name _____ Date _____

Practicing Handy Facts

Solve the following problems. Use your multiplication table when you need help.

1. $3 \times 2 =$ _____ 2. $6 \times 10 =$ _____ 3. $0 \times 10 =$ _____

4. $6 \times 5 =$ _____ 5. $8 \times 10 =$ _____ 6. $7 \times 1 =$ _____

7. $4 \times 1 =$ _____ 8. $9 \times 3 =$ _____ 9. $6 \times 2 =$ _____

10. $1 \times 4 =$ _____ 11. $9 \times 5 =$ _____ 12. $5 \times 5 =$ _____

13. 7
    ×5

14. 7
    ×2

15. 8
    ×5

16. 3
    ×3

17. 3
    ×5

18. 6
    ×0

19. 0
    ×2

20. 1
    ×3

21. 4
    ×5

22. 2
    ×3

23. 2
    ×5

24. 5
    ×2

Write and solve a multiplication story about zero. Write a number sentence to go with it.

_____

_____

_____

_____

Handy Facts   DAB • Grade 3 • Unit 11 • Lesson 2 **161**

Discovery Assignment Book - page 161

Discovery Assignment Book (p. 161)

Practicing Handy Facts

1. 6   2. 60
3. 0   4. 30
5. 80   6. 7
7. 4   8. 27
9. 12   10. 4
11. 45   12. 25
13. 35   14. 14
15. 40   16. 9
17. 15   18. 0
19. 0   20. 3
21. 20   22. 6
23. 10   24. 10

Discovery Assignment Book (p. 163)

Nickels and Dimes

1.

Number of Nickels	Number of Dimes	Value of Nickels	Value of Dimes	Total Value
5	3	$.25	$.30	$.55
7	2	$.35	$.20	$.55
8	4	$.40	$.40	$.80
6	8	$.30	$.80	$1.10
2	9	$.10	$.90	$1.00
4	10	$.20	$1.00	$1.20
3	3	$.15	$.30	$.45
1	5	$.05	$.50	$.55
0	7	0	$.70	$.70
9	1	$.45	$.10	$.55

Name _____ Date _____

Nickels and Dimes

Homework

1. Complete the following table by counting money (real or pretend) or by using arithmetic.

Number of Nickels	Number of Dimes	Value of Nickels	Value of Dimes	Total Value
5	3	$.25	$.30	$.55
7	2			
	4	$.40		
	8	$.30		
2			$.90	
4			$1.00	
3			$.30	$.45
		$.05	$.50	
0	7			
9			$.10	$.55

Handy Facts   DAB • Grade 3 • Unit 11 • Lesson 2 **163**

Discovery Assignment Book - page 163

Discovery Assignment Book (p. 164)

2.

Number of Nickels	Number of Dimes	Value of Nickels	Value of Dimes	Total Value
1	4	$.05	$.40	$.45
3	3	$.15	$.30	$.45
5	2	$.25	$.20	$.45
7	1	$.35	$.10	$.45

Name _____ Date _____

2. How many ways can you make $.45 using only nickels and dimes? List them in the table below.

Number of Nickels	Number of Dimes	Value of Nickels	Value of Dimes	Total Value

164 DAB • Grade 3 • Unit 11 • Lesson 2   Handy Facts

Discovery Assignment Book - page 164

Lesson 3

Multiplication and Rectangles

Lesson Overview

Estimated Class Sessions

2

Students arrange square-inch tiles into rectangles to find factors of 6, 12, and 18. They turn the rectangles around and learn that changing the order of the factors in a multiplication sentence does not change the product (e.g., $3 \times 6 = 18$ and $6 \times 3 = 18$). They build squares with their tiles to derive the square number multiplication facts and look for patterns among square numbers. They record new facts on their multiplication tables. Finally, they solve problems about tile arrangements.

Key Content

- Representing multiplication using rectangular arrays.
- Deriving turn-around facts.
- Investigating square and prime numbers.
- Solving problems involving multiplication and division.

Key Vocabulary

- array
- column of an array
- prime number
- row of an array
- square number
- turn-around fact

Math Facts

DPP Bit E provides practice multiplying with 0 and 1. Task F is multiplication fact practice.

Homework

Assign the Tile Problems Homework section on the *Multiplication and Rectangles* Activity Pages.

Assessment

Use *Questions 3–4* of the Homework section for an assessment.

Materials List

Supplies and Copies

Student	Teacher
Supplies for Each Student	**Supplies**
• 25 square-inch tiles of one color	
Copies	**Copies/Transparencies**
• 2 copies of *Centimeter Grid Paper* per student (*Unit Resource Guide* Page 52)	• 1 transparency of *Centimeter Grid Paper* (*Unit Resource Guide* Page 52)
• 1 copy of *Three-column Data Table* per student, optional (*Unit Resource Guide* Page 53)	• 1 transparency of *My Multiplication Table* with the 0, 1, 2, 3, 5, and 10 columns completed (*Discovery Assignment Book* Page 159)
• 1 copy of *Square-Inch Grid Paper* per student (*Unit Resource Guide* Page 54)	
• 1 copy of *My Multiplication Table* with the 0, 1, 2, 3, 5, and 10 columns completed per student (*Discovery Assignment Book* Page 159)	

All blackline masters including assessment, transparency, and DPP masters are also on the Teacher Resource CD.

Student Books
Multiplication and Rectangles (*Student Guide* Pages 145–148)

Daily Practice and Problems and Home Practice
DPP items E–H (*Unit Resource Guide* Pages 19–20)

Note: Classrooms whose pacing differs significantly from the suggested pacing of the units should use the Math Facts Calendar in Section 4 of the *Facts Resource Guide* to ensure students receive the complete math facts program.

Daily Practice and Problems

Suggestions for using the DPPs are on page 50.

E. Bit: Multiplication Facts:
0s and 1s (URG p. 19)

A. $5 \times 0 =$ B. $5 \times 1 =$

C. $10 \times 0 =$ D. $1 \times 10 =$

E. $0 \times 47 =$ F. $47 \times 1 =$

G. $0 \times 736 =$ H. $1 \times 736 =$

I. Use your calculator to check your answers.

J. What can you say about multiplying numbers by 0?

K. What can you say about multiplying numbers by 1?

F. Task: More Fives and Tens
(URG p. 19)

A. $5 \times 3 =$ B. $10 \times 3 =$

C. $5 \times 5 =$ D. $10 \times 5 =$

E. $5 \times 7 =$ F. $10 \times 7 =$

G. $5 \times 9 =$ H. $10 \times 9 =$

What patterns do you see?

G. Bit: Counting by Fives (URG p. 19)

1. Count by 5-minute periods from 1:00 to 2:00. Make a list.

2. How many 5-minute periods are there from 1:00 to 2:00?

3. How many 5-minute periods are there in two hours?

H. Task: Story Solving (URG p. 20)

Write a story and draw a picture about $5 \times \frac{1}{4}$.
Write a number sentence for your picture.

Teaching the Activity

Questions 1–3 on the *Multiplication and Rectangles* Activity Pages in the *Student Guide* summarize for students the steps in exploring the factors of 6 with tiles. You may prefer to lead the activity without using the *Student Guide.* Ask students:

* *Arrange six tiles into rectangles in as many ways as you can.*

Students should work individually and then compare their rectangles with a partner's. Students should find four ways to arrange the six tiles, counting the arrangement of two rows and three columns, for example, as different from the arrangement of three rows and two columns. Explain that **rows** are horizontal and **columns** are vertical. Ask:

* *How many rows and columns do you see in this rectangle?*
* *Can you think of a number sentence to match this rectangle?*

Student Guide - page 145

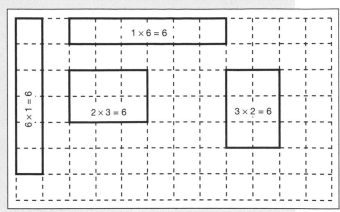

Figure 4: *Four rectangles made with six tiles*

After you demonstrate this on the transparency, have students draw their rectangles on *Centimeter Grid Paper* and write multiplication sentences inside them, as in Figure 4. If students suggest number sentences using repeated addition (e.g., 2 + 2 + 2), link this with multiplication by showing how both number sentences match the rectangle. Emphasize that students will write multiplication sentences. This procedure should be repeated for 12 and 18 tiles in *Questions 4–5*.

In *Question 6,* students discover that the numbers 5 and 7 each have only two factors, themselves and 1. Tell them that numbers with this property are called **prime.** The only rectangles that can be made using a prime number of tiles are those with only one row or column. Ask the students to find other prime numbers by building rectangles.

In working with the tiles, students will find that multiplication is commutative—although this term is not used at this point. For *Questions 8–9,* students use the commutative property to get new facts from old by "turning around" the facts they already found. Help students to see that a fact such as 9 × 3 = 27, which appears in column 3 on the *My Multiplication Table* Activity Page, is a **turn-around fact** for 3 × 9 = 27, which they can enter in row 3. The turn-around facts for any column in the table are in the corresponding row—for example, row 3 and column 3 have the same entries.

Exploring Factors of 6 Using Tiles

1. Arrange 6 square tiles into rectangles in as many ways as you can.
2. Draw your rectangles on *Centimeter Grid Paper.*
3. Write multiplication sentences inside each rectangle.

Exploring Factors of 12 and 18 Using Tiles

4. Arrange 12 tiles into rectangles in as many ways as you can. Then draw your rectangles on graph paper. Write multiplication sentences inside each rectangle.
5. Do the same thing with 18 tiles.

Exploring Factors of 5 and 7 Using Tiles

6. Arrange 5 and 7 tiles into rectangles in as many ways as you can.
7. How are the rectangles you can make for 5 and 7 different from the ones you can make for 6, 12, and 18?

Exploring Turn-around Facts

8. Choose a multiplication fact, and turn its factors around. For example, 2 × 3 = 6 can be turned around to make 3 × 2 = ____ . Make a rectangle to match your new fact.

2 × 3 = 6

3 × 2 = 6

9. We call the facts that we get from known ones in this way **turn-around facts.** Record in your multiplication table all facts that are turn-around facts for the ones you've already recorded.

Student Guide - page 146 *(Answers on p. 55)*

TIMS Tip

Connecting a number sentence with a picture may not be apparent to some students. Emphasize that number sentences must match the picture. Give students examples of number sentences that do not match a picture. For example, for a 5 × 4 array, students may write 2 × 10 = 20. Even though the product is the same, the number sentence does not match the picture. Point out that students should count the number of rows and columns in the rectangle.

For *Questions 10–12,* students build squares with their tiles to derive the squares of the numbers from 1 to 10. On a separate sheet of paper or a *Three-column Data Table* students make a table of squares similar to the one shown for *Question 10.* Then they record the square facts on their multiplication tables. Students may notice that the square numbers run diagonally left to right through the multiplication table.

Figure 5 shows the facts they should have entered in their tables after completing *Questions 8–12.*

×	0	1	2	3	4	5	6	7	8	9	10
0	0	0	0	0	0	0	0	0	0	0	0
1	0	1	2	3	4	5	6	7	8	9	10
2	0	2	4	6	8	10	12	14	16	18	20
3	0	3	6	9	12	15	18	21	24	27	30
4	0	4	8	12	16	20					40
5	0	5	10	15	20	25	30	35	40	45	50
6	0	6	12	18		30	36				60
7	0	7	14	21		35		49			70
8	0	8	16	24		40			64		80
9	0	9	18	27		45				81	90
10	0	10	20	30	40	50	60	70	80	90	100

Figure 5: *The multiplication table as filled in during this activity*

Exploring Square Numbers

10. Use your tiles to build squares of different sizes, up to at least 10 × 10. Count the number of tiles on each side and the total number of tiles in each square. Make a table like this one.

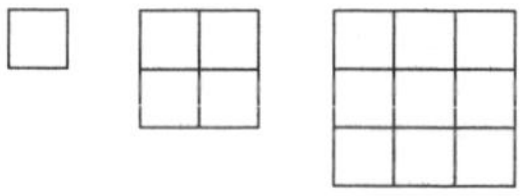

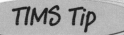

Number on a Side	Number in Square	Multiplication Facts
1	1	1 × 1 = 1
2	4	2 × 2 = 4
3	9	

11. The numbers 1, 4, 9, and so on are called **square numbers.** Enter your facts from Question 10 about square numbers in your multiplication table.

12. Do you see a pattern for square numbers?

Multiplication and Rectangles   SG • Grade 3 • Unit 11 • Lesson 3   147

Student Guide - page 147 *(Answers on p. 56)*

TIMS Tip

If each student has 25 tiles, he or she can build his or her own small squares, but will need to combine tiles with other students to get the 100 tiles needed to build the large squares.

Math Facts

DPP Bit E provides practice multiplying with 0 and 1. Task F provides practice with the multiplication facts for the fives and tens.

Homework and Practice

- Assign the Homework section in the *Student Guide.* Instead of sending tiles home, send home a sheet of *Square-Inch Grid Paper* and have the students cut it into "tiles."

- For DPP Bit G students skip count by 5-minute periods. Task H explores multiplying a fraction by a whole number.

Assessment

Use Homework **Questions 3–4** to assess students' abilities to solve problems using arrays and to write number sentences for them.

Extension

- **Prime numbers.** Ask students to use tiles to investigate the factors of the numbers 1 to 50 and to identify the prime numbers. You might want to assign a different set of numbers to each group so their findings can be combined into a comprehensive class list.

- **Square numbers.** Ask students to make a list of square numbers: 0, 1, 4, 9, 16, 25, 36, 49. . . . Then ask them to subtract consecutive square numbers and to make a list of the differences. The first few numbers in the list of differences are 1 $(1 - 0)$, 3 $(4 - 1)$, and 5 $(9 - 4)$. Pose questions like these:

  1. *What pattern do you see?* (The squares go up by consecutive odd numbers.)

  2. *Does this pattern continue?* (Yes)

  3. *Can you use this pattern to predict the next square number?* (Yes, $16 = 9 + 7$)

Literature Connection

- Hulme, Joy N. *Sea Squares.* Hyperion Books for Children, New York, 1993.

This book develops square number facts through counting.

At a Glance

Math Facts and Daily Practice and Problems

DPP Bit E provides practice multiplying with 0 and 1. Task F is multiplication fact practice. Bit G involves time. Task H explores fraction concepts.

Teaching the Activity

1. Demonstrate how rectangular arrays can represent multiplication facts.
2. Students complete *Questions 1–5* on the *Multiplication and Rectangles* Activity Pages in the *Student Guide.* They arrange tiles into rectangles and write number sentences to describe the rectangles.
3. Students answer *Questions 6–7* and learn about prime numbers.
4. For *Questions 8–9,* students learn that multiplication is commutative. They enter turn-around facts for the facts they found on the *My Multiplication Table* Activity Page in the *Discovery Assignment Book.*
5. For *Questions 10–12* on the *Multiplication and Rectangles* Activity Pages, students use tiles to find the squares of numbers from 1 to 10. They make a table of squares and record the square facts on the *My Multiplication Table* Activity Page.

Homework

Assign the Tile Problems Homework section on the *Multiplication and Rectangles* Activity Pages.

Assessment

Use *Questions 3–4* of the Homework section for an assessment.

Extension

1. Have students use tiles to identify the prime numbers between 1 and 50.
2. Have students make a list of the square numbers. Then have them subtract consecutive square numbers and explore the patterns.

Connection

Read and discuss *Sea Squares* by Joy Hulme.

Answer Key is on pages 55–56.

Notes:

Name _____ Date _____

Centimeter Grid Paper, Blackline Master

Name _____   Date _____

_____

Name _____ Date _____

Square-Inch Grid Paper, Blackline Master

Student Guide (p. 146)

1.–3.* See Figure 3 in the Lesson Guide.

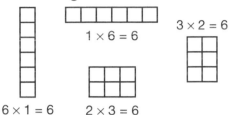

$1 \times 6 = 6$

$3 \times 2 = 6$

$6 \times 1 = 6$

$2 \times 3 = 6$

4.

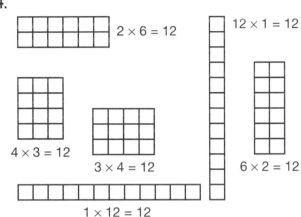

$2 \times 6 = 12$

$12 \times 1 = 12$

$4 \times 3 = 12$

$3 \times 4 = 12$

$6 \times 2 = 12$

$1 \times 12 = 12$

5.

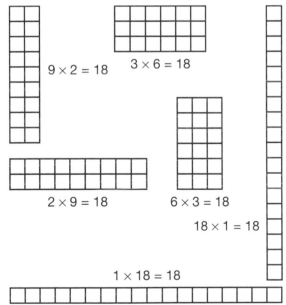

$9 \times 2 = 18$

$3 \times 6 = 18$

$2 \times 9 = 18$

$6 \times 3 = 18$

$18 \times 1 = 18$

$1 \times 18 = 18$

Exploring Factors of 6 Using Tiles

1. Arrange 6 square tiles into rectangles in as many ways as you can.
2. Draw your rectangles on *Centimeter Grid Paper.*
3. Write multiplication sentences inside each rectangle.

Exploring Factors of 12 and 18 Using Tiles

4. Arrange 12 tiles into rectangles in as many ways as you can. Then draw your rectangles on graph paper. Write multiplication sentences inside each rectangle.
5. Do the same thing with 18 tiles.

Exploring Factors of 5 and 7 Using Tiles

6. Arrange 5 and 7 tiles into rectangles in as many ways as you can.
7. How are the rectangles you can make for 5 and 7 different from the ones you can make for 6, 12, and 18?

Exploring Turn-around Facts

8. Choose a multiplication fact, and turn its factors around. For example, $2 \times 3 = 6$ can be turned around to make $3 \times 2 =$ _____ . Make a rectangle to match your new fact.

$2 \times 3 = 6$

$3 \times 2 = 6$

9. We call the facts that we get from known ones in this way **turn-around facts**. Record in your multiplication table all facts that are turn-around facts for the ones you've already recorded.

146   SG • Grade 3 • Unit 11 • Lesson 3   Multiplication and Rectangles

Student Guide - page 146

6.*

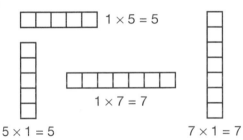

$1 \times 5 = 5$

$1 \times 7 = 7$

$5 \times 1 = 5$

$7 \times 1 = 7$

7. Using 5 or 7 tiles you can make only two rectangles. When using 6, 12, or 18 tiles, you can form 4 or 6 different rectangles.

8. Answers will vary.*

9. At this time, in addition to the starred columns, the following rows should be completed on the *My Multiplication Table* Activity Page in the *Discovery Assignment Book:* 0s, 1s, 2s, 3s, 5s, and 10s.*

---

*Answers and/or discussion are included in the Lesson Guide.

Student Guide - page 147

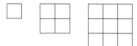

Exploring Square Numbers

10. Use your tiles to build squares of different sizes, up to at least 10 × 10. Count the number of tiles on each side and the total number of tiles in each square. Make a table like this one.

Number on a Side	Number in Square	Multiplication Facts
1	1	1 × 1 = 1
2	4	2 × 2 = 4
3	9	

11. The numbers 1, 4, 9, and so on are called **square numbers.** Enter your facts from Question 10 about square numbers in your multiplication table.

12. Do you see a pattern for square numbers?

Multiplication and Rectangles   SG • Grade 3 • Unit 11 • Lesson 3   **147**

Student Guide - page 147

(Homework)

Tile Problems

Use tiles or grid paper to help you solve these problems. Write a number sentence to go with each problem.

1. Sam made a rectangle with 30 tiles. If there were 6 rows, how many were in each row?

2. Julia made a rectangle with 7 rows and 5 in each row. How many tiles did she use?

3. Sara made an array with 24 tiles. There were 8 tiles in each row. How many rows were there?

4. A rectangle of 12 tiles has tiles of 3 different colors. There is an equal number of tiles of each color. How many tiles of each color are there?

5. Arrange 20 tiles into rectangles in as many ways as you can. Write a number sentence for each rectangle.

6. Arrange 11 tiles into rectangles in as many ways as you can. Write a number sentence for each rectangle.

148 SG • Grade 3 • Unit 11 • Lesson 3   Multiplication and Rectangles

Student Guide - page 148

Student Guide (p. 147)

10.

Number on a Side	Number in Square	Multiplication Facts
1	1	1 × 1 = 1
2	4	2 × 2 = 4
3	9	3 × 3 = 9
4	16	4 × 4 = 16
5	25	5 × 5 = 25
6	36	6 × 6 = 36
7	49	7 × 7 = 49
8	64	8 × 8 = 64
9	81	9 × 9 = 81
10	100	10 × 10 = 100

11. See Figure 5 in the Lesson Guide. The facts from the table above should be added to the *My Multiplication Table* Activity Page in the *Discovery Assignment Book.***

12. Answers will vary. The difference between the squares goes up by consecutive odd numbers. The square numbers run diagonally upper left to lower right through the multiplication table. See the Extension section in the Lesson Guide.*

Student Guide (p. 148)

Homework

Number sentences may vary.

1. 5 tiles; 6 × 5 = 30 tiles

2. 35 tiles; 7 × 5 = 35 tiles

3. 3 rows; 24 ÷ 8 = 3 rows

4. 4 tiles; 12 ÷ 3 = 4 tiles

5. 1 × 20 = 20, 20 × 1 = 20,
2 × 10 = 20, 10 × 2 = 20,
4 × 5 = 20, 5 × 4 = 20

6. 11 × 1 = 11, 1 × 11 = 11

*Answers and/or discussion are included in the Lesson Guide.

Lesson 4

Completing the Table

Lesson Overview

Estimated Class Sessions

2

In Part 1, students complete their multiplication tables by finding the remaining multiplication facts through skip counting or using a calculator. Symmetry in the table is discussed as well as patterns for multiples of 9. In Part 2, students learn how to use the *Triangle Flash Cards: 5s* and *10s* to practice the facts. They begin their *Multiplication Facts I Know* charts.

Key Content

- Identifying patterns for multiples of nine.
- Investigating symmetry in the multiplication table.

Key Vocabulary

- symmetry

Math Facts

DPP items J and L provide practice with multiplication facts.

Homework

1. Assign the Homework section of the *Completing the Table* Activity Pages.
2. Students take home their lists of facts they need to study and the *Triangle Flash Cards* to practice the facts with a family member.
3. Assign Parts 1 and 2 of the Home Practice.

Curriculum Sequence

Before This Unit

In Units 2–10, students reviewed and were assessed on the subtraction facts primarily through the Daily Practice and Problems. They also developed strategies for the multiplication facts.

After This Unit

In Units 12–20, students will continue to practice and assess the multiplication facts. In each unit, they will study a small group of facts in the Daily Practice and Problems. In Grade 4 students will review the multiplication facts and develop fluency with the division facts.

Materials List

Supplies and Copies

Student	Teacher
Supplies for Each Student • calculator, optional • envelope for storing flash cards	**Supplies**
Copies • 2 *Small Multiplication Tables* (1 for class and 1 for home) per student, optional (*Unit Resource Guide* Page 67) • 1 copy of *My Multiplication Table,* completed in Lessons 2 and 3 per student (*Discovery Assignment Book* Page 159)	**Copies/Transparencies** • 1 transparency of *My Multiplication Table,* completed in Lessons 2 and 3 (*Discovery Assignment Book* Page 159) • 1 transparency of *Multiplication Table* (*Unit Resource Guide* Page 66)

All blackline masters including assessment, transparency, and DPP masters are also on the Teacher Resource CD.

Student Books

Completing the Table (*Student Guide* Pages 149–151)
Triangle Flash Cards: 5s (*Discovery Assignment Book* Page 165)
Triangle Flash Cards: 10s (*Discovery Assignment Book* Page 167)
Multiplication Facts I Know (*Discovery Assignment Book* Page 169)

Daily Practice and Problems and Home Practice

DPP items I–L (*Unit Resource Guide* Pages 20–21)
Home Practice Parts 1–2 (*Discovery Assignment Book* Page 156)

Note: Classrooms whose pacing differs significantly from the suggested pacing of the units should use the Math Facts Calendar in Section 4 of the *Facts Resource Guide* to ensure students receive the complete math facts program.

Daily Practice and Problems

Suggestions for using the DPPs are on page 64.

I. Bit: Lizardland Picnic (URG p. 20)

At Lizardland, eight people can sit at a table in Picnic Park. If your class had a picnic there (including your teacher), how many tables would you need? Draw a picture to show your answer.

K. Bit: Cookies (URG p. 21)

At Max and Cora's cookie stand, one cookie costs 35¢. How many different ways can you pay exact change for one cookie using only nickels, dimes, and quarters?

J. Task: Nickels and Dimes
(URG p. 20)

You may use real or pretend money to help you solve the following problems.

1. What is the total value of 6 nickels and 4 dimes?
2. A. The total value of 55¢ is made up of 2 dimes and how many nickels?
   B. Name three other ways you can make 55¢ using only nickels and dimes.

L. Task: More Nickels and Dimes
(URG p. 21)

True or false? Explain how you know.

1. 4 dimes < 6 nickels
2. 7 dimes and 4 nickels = 9 dimes
3. 15 nickels > 6 dimes

Part 1 Patterns for Nine

The *Completing the Table* Activity Pages in the *Student Guide* begin by pointing out that students only need to find a few more facts to complete their multiplication tables. Remind them that when they find a fact, such as 4 × 6, they can also record its turn-around fact, 6 × 4. When students begin the lesson, they should have 20 blank squares left (from the original 121) in their multiplication tables. Because of the turn-around rule of multiplication, they actually have only 10 facts remaining.

Have students figure out the remaining facts in any manner they wish. Some good strategies include using skip counting, a calculator, a number line, or counters. Another good strategy is to use known facts to derive the new ones. For example, a student might add to the known fact 5 × 4 = 20 to derive the new fact 6 × 4 = 24:

"I know that 5 × 4 = 20. So, 6 × 4 is 4 more—24." A student might subtract from the known fact 5 × 8 = 40 to derive the new fact 4 × 8 = 32: "I know that 5 × 8 is 40. So, 4 × 8 is 8 less—32."

After completing their multiplication tables, students look for patterns in their tables. They have already looked for patterns in earlier activities, but will probably see new ones in the completed table.

Question 1 asks students to look for patterns with nines. In discovering patterns in *Question 2*, students might observe the following:

1. When the products are listed in a column, as below, it is easy to see that the digits in the ten's place count up by ones (0, 1, 2, 3 . . .) and that the digits in the one's place count down by ones (9, 8, 7 . . .).

    9
   18
   27
   36
   45
   54
   63
   72
   81

Completing the Table

You should have only 20 blank squares left in your multiplication table. Use any strategy you like—skip counting, a calculator, a number line, or counters—to find the remaining facts.

When you find a fact, such as 4 × 6, you can also record its turn-around fact—in this case, 6 × 4.

Patterns for Nine

1. Copy and complete the list of facts for 9. Then write the products in a column, one on each line.

   0 × 9 = ?

   1 × 9 = ?

   2 × 9 = ?

   3 × 9 = ?

   4 × 9 = ?

   5 × 9 = ?

   6 × 9 = ?

   7 × 9 = ?

   8 × 9 = ?

   9 × 9 = ?

2. What patterns do you see in your list?

Completing the Table   SG • Grade 3 • Unit 11 • Lesson 4 149

Student Guide - page 149 (Answers on p. 68)

TIMS Tip

To remember 9s facts it often helps to see how simple it is to derive them from the familiar 10s facts. For example, "10 × 4 is 40. So, 9 × 4 is 4 less: 40 − 4 = 36" and "10 × 5 is 50. So, 9 × 5 is 5 less: 50 − 5 = 45."

3. Use your calculator to find the products below. Then add the digits in each product. Repeat adding the digits until you get a one digit number.

   Example: 9 × 634 = 5706   5 + 7 + 0 + 6 = 18   1 + 8 = 9

   A. 9 × 47   **B.** 9 × 83
   C. 9 × 89   **D.** 9 × 92
   E. 9 × 123   **F.** 9 × 633
   G. 9 × 697   **H.** 9 × 333

4. Describe what happens when you add the digits of a multiple of 9.

Multiplication Facts and Triangle Flash Cards

Practice multiplication facts with a partner. Use your *Triangle Flash Cards: 5s* and *Triangle Flash Cards: 10s*, and follow the directions below.

- One partner covers the shaded number, the largest number on the card. This number will be the answer to the multiplication problem. It is called the **product.**

5 × 4 = ?

4 × 5 = ?

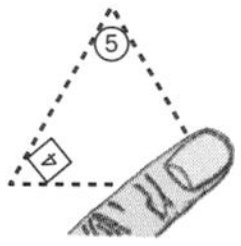

- The second person multiplies the two uncovered numbers (one in a circle, one in a square). These are the two **factors.** It doesn't matter which of the factors is said first. 4 × 5 and 5 × 4 both equal 20.
- Divide the cards into three piles: those facts you know and can answer quickly, those you can figure out with a strategy, and those you need to learn.

150 SG • Grade 3 • Unit 11 • Lesson 4   Completing the Table

Student Guide* - page 150 *(Answers on p. 68)

Name ______________________ Date ______________

Multiplication Facts I Know

- **Circle the facts you know well.**
- **Keep this table and use it to help you multiply.**
- **As you learn more facts, you may circle them too.**

×	0	1	2	3	4	5	6	7	8	9	10
0	0	0	0	0	0	0	0	0	0	0	0
1	0	1	2	3	4	5	6	7	8	9	10
2	0	2	4	6	8	10	12	14	16	18	20
3	0	3	6	9	12	15	18	21	24	27	30
4	0	4	8	12	16	20	24	28	32	36	40
5	0	5	10	15	20	25	30	35	40	45	50
6	0	6	12	18	24	30	36	42	48	54	60
7	0	7	14	21	28	35	42	49	56	63	70
8	0	8	16	24	32	40	48	56	64	72	80
9	0	9	18	27	36	45	54	63	72	81	90
10	0	10	20	30	40	50	60	70	80	90	100

Completing the Table   DAB • Grade 3 • Unit 11 • Lesson 4 169

***Discovery Assignment Book* - page 169**

2. The sums of the two digits in each of the products listed is nine. For example, 3 + 6 = 9 and 7 + 2 = 9. In fact, the sum of the digits of any multiple of 9 is also a multiple of 9. Furthermore, the process of adding digits can be repeated until nine itself results. As illustrated in ***Question 3,*** 9 × 634 = 5706. Adding the product's digits provides a multiple of nine: 5 + 7 + 0 + 6 = 18. Adding the new answer's digits results in nine: 1 + 8 = 9. In ***Question 3,*** students work with other multiples of nine to discover that this pattern is consistent.

Students may notice other patterns in their multiplication tables. They may notice that the diagonal line from the top left corner to the bottom right corner is a line of symmetry formed by the square numbers. To see this, students can circle a number above the line and connect it to its matching number on the bottom half, as in Figure 6.

×	0	1	2	3	4	5	6	7	8	9	10
0	0	0	0	0	0	0	0	0	0	0	0
1	0	1	2	3	4	5	6	7	8	9	10
2	0	2	4	6	8	10	12	14	16	18	20
3	0	3	6	9	12	15	18	21	24	27	30
4	0	4	8	12	16	20	24	28	32	36	40
5	0	5	10	15	20	25	30	35	40	45	50
6	0	6	12	18	24	30	36	42	48	54	60
7	0	7	14	21	28	35	42	49	56	63	70
8	0	8	16	24	32	40	48	56	64	72	80
9	0	9	18	27	36	45	54	63	72	81	90
10	0	10	20	30	40	50	60	70	80	90	100

Figure 6: *Symmetry in the multiplication table*

TIMS Tip

Adding the digits of the product of a 9s fact to see whether they add up to nine can be a strategy for remembering 9s facts. For example, a student might think, "Let me see, does 9 × 6 equal 54 or 56? It must be 54 since 5 + 4 is 9, but 5 + 6 is not 9."

Journal Prompt

Describe the patterns in your multiplication table.

Part 2 Multiplication Facts and Triangle Flash Cards

The *Triangle Flash Cards: 5s* and *Triangle Flash Cards: 10s* are located in the *Discovery Assignment Book.* The *Student Guide* outlines how students use the *Triangle Flash Cards* for practicing the multiplication facts. Partners cover the number that is shaded (the largest number on the card). This is the **product,** the answer to the multiplication problem that the other two numbers—the **factors**—present. The student being quizzed multiplies the two numbers showing, gives the answer, and the answer is checked.

As their partners quiz them on the facts, students sort the cards into three piles—those facts they can answer quickly, those they know using a strategy, and those they need to learn. Then each student begins a *Multiplication Facts I Know* chart found in the *Discovery Assignment Book.* Students circle the facts they know and can answer quickly on the chart. Remind students that if they know a fact, they also know its turn-around fact. So if they circle $5 \times 3 = 15$, they can also circle $3 \times 5 = 15$.

Review with students what they learned in Lesson 2 about multiplication by zero and one. Students can also circle these facts.

Students list the facts they did not circle on their charts. They take this list home along with their flash cards to practice the facts they need to study with a family member. Students will take a quiz on the multiplication facts for the fives and tens in DPP Bit S at the end of this unit. After the quiz, they update their charts.

As students encounter multiplication problems with the facts in the activities and labs, encourage them to share their strategies. The fives and tens are easily solved using skip counting. For descriptions of other multiplication facts strategies, see the TIMS Tutor: *Math Facts* in the *Teacher Implementation Guide.*

Instruct students to keep their *Multiplication Facts I Know* charts in a safe place. They will use the charts to track their progress learning the multiplication facts as they continue to study them in Units 12–20.

TIMS Tip

Use the *Small Multiplication Tables* Page to make a small multiplication table for each student. (There are four tables on each page.) Students can tape them to their desks or notebooks for easy reference so they have ready access to all the facts while they are working on activities or playing games.

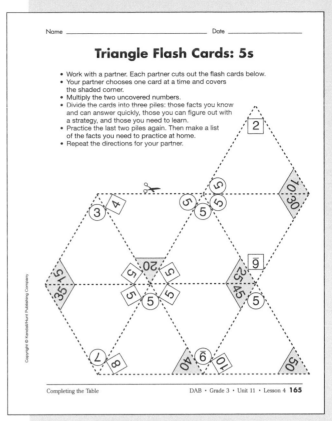

Discovery Assignment Book - page 165

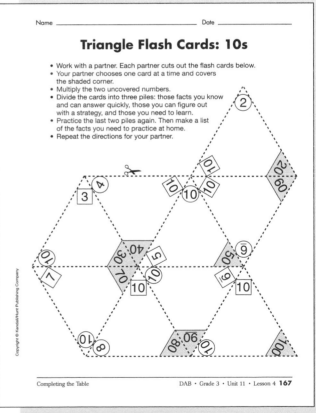

Discovery Assignment Book - page 167

- Discuss how you can figure out facts that you do not recall right away. Share your strategies with your partner.
- Practice the last two piles again. Then make a list of the facts you need to practice at home for homework.
- Circle the facts you know quickly on your *Multiplication Facts I Know* chart. Remember that if you know one fact, you also know its turn-around fact. Circle both on your chart.

Multiplication Facts I Know

×	0	1	2	3	4	5	6	7	8	9	10
0	0	0	0	0	0	0	0	0	0	0	0
1	0	1	2	3	4	5	6	7	8	9	10
2	0	2	4	6	8	10	12	14	16	18	20
3	0	3	6	9	12	15	18	21	24	27	30
4	0	4	8	12	16	20	24	28	32	36	40
5	0	5	10	15	20	25	30	35	40	45	50
6	0	6	12	18	24	30	36	42	48	54	60
7	0	7	14	21	28	35	42	49	56	63	70
8	0	8	16	24	32	40	48	56	64	72	80
9	0	9	18	27	36	45	54	63	72	81	90
10	0	10	20	30	40	50	60	70	80	90	100

Homework

Find these products.

1. $3 \times 4 = ?$
2. $6 \times 7 = ?$
3. $6 \times 5 = ?$
4. $5 \times 4 = ?$
5. $7 \times 9 = ?$
6. $4 \times 2 = ?$
7. $8 \times 5 = ?$
8. $8 \times 8 = ?$
9. $7 \times 4 = ?$
10. $0 \times 6 = ?$
11. $7 \times 3 = ?$
12. $9 \times 6 = ?$
13. $6 \times 8 = ?$
14. $7 \times 8 = ?$
15. $9 \times 9 = ?$

16. $\begin{array}{r} 7 \\ \times 5 \\ \hline \end{array}$
17. $\begin{array}{r} 6 \\ \times 9 \\ \hline \end{array}$
18. $\begin{array}{r} 3 \\ \times 8 \\ \hline \end{array}$

19. $\begin{array}{r} 4 \\ \times 6 \\ \hline \end{array}$
20. $\begin{array}{r} 8 \\ \times 3 \\ \hline \end{array}$
21. $\begin{array}{r} 9 \\ \times 1 \\ \hline \end{array}$

22. $\begin{array}{r} 8 \\ \times 4 \\ \hline \end{array}$
23. $\begin{array}{r} 6 \\ \times 6 \\ \hline \end{array}$
24. $\begin{array}{r} 7 \\ \times 7 \\ \hline \end{array}$

25. Choose one of the facts in Questions 1–24. Write a multiplication story about it. Draw a picture to go with your story.

Completing the Table   SG · Grade 3 · Unit 11 · Lesson 4   **151**

Math Facts

DPP items J and L provide practice with the multiplication facts for the fives and tens using problems with nickels and dimes.

Homework and Practice

- Assign the Homework section in the *Student Guide.* Allow students to take home their completed multiplication tables.
- DPP Bit I builds number sense through a division word problem. Bit K is a problem involving money.
- Remind students to practice the multiplication facts for the fives and tens throughout the rest of this unit using their *Triangle Flash Cards.*
- Parts 1 and 2 of the Home Practice can be assigned for homework. They provide addition and subtraction practice.

Answers for Parts 1 and 2 of the Home Practice are in the Answer Key at the end of this lesson and at the end of this unit.

Name _____ Date _____

Unit 11 Home Practice

PART 1

1. $160 - 70 =$ _____
2. $120 - 50 =$ _____
3. $140 - 60 =$ _____
4. $82 +$ _____ $= 100$
5. $53 +$ _____ $= 100$
6. $44 +$ _____ $= 100$

7. When Tony cleaned his mom's car he found some coins under the seats. His mom let him keep the coins and gave him $.25 more for cleaning the car. Now he has $2.00.
   A. How much money did Tony find in the car? _____
   B. What coins and how many of each could he have found? Give two possible answers.

PART 2

1. $600 + 700 =$ _____
2. $400 + 800 =$ _____
3. $500 + 900 =$ _____
4. $1000 -$ _____ $= 450$
5. $1000 -$ _____ $= 343$

6. Tina's high school graduating class has 321 students. Rita's junior high graduating class has 132 students. Sara, who is graduating from kindergarten, is in a class of 42 students.
   A. How many more students are in Tina's class than in Rita's?

   B. If all three classes attend the same ceremony, how many students would be graduating?

156 DAB · Grade 3 · Unit 11   MULTIPLICATION PATTERNS

Discovery Assignment Book - page 156 (Answers on p. 69)

At a Glance

Math Facts and Daily Practice and Problems

Bits I and K are word problems. DPP items J and L provide practice with multiplication facts.

Part 1. Patterns for Nines

1. Using any method they choose, students fill in ten of the blank spaces on *My Multiplication Table* for Lessons 2 and 3.
2. Students use turn-around facts to fill in the remaining blank spaces.
3. Students look for patterns with multiples of nine and discuss using the patterns to learn the facts.
4. Students look for symmetry in their multiplication tables. Use the *Multiplication Table* Transparency Master to model the table's symmetry.
5. Students complete *Questions 1–4* of the *Completing the Table* Activity Pages in the *Student Guide.*

Part 2. Multiplication Facts and Triangle Flash Cards

1. Following the directions in the *Student Guide,* students practice the facts for the fives and tens using *Triangle Flash Cards.*
2. Students sort their cards into three piles according to how well they know each fact. They begin their *Multiplication Facts I Know* charts by circling the facts they know well and can answer quickly.
3. Students list the fives and tens they still need to learn.
4. Students review multiplication by zero and one and circle these facts on their charts.

Homework

1. Assign the Homework section of the *Completing the Table* Activity Pages.
2. Students take home their lists of facts they need to study and the *Triangle Flash Cards* to practice the facts with a family member.
3. Assign Parts 1 and 2 of the Home Practice.

Answer Key is on pages 68–69.

Notes:

Multiplication Table

×	0	1	2	3	4	5	6	7	8	9	10
0	0	0	0	0	0	0	0	0	0	0	0
1	0	1	2	3	4	5	6	7	8	9	10
2	0	2	4	6	8	10	12	14	16	18	20
3	0	3	6	9	12	15	18	21	24	27	30
4	0	4	8	12	16	20	24	28	32	36	40
5	0	5	10	15	20	25	30	35	40	45	50
6	0	6	12	18	24	30	36	42	48	54	60
7	0	7	14	21	28	35	42	49	56	63	70
8	0	8	16	24	32	40	48	56	64	72	80
9	0	9	18	27	36	45	54	63	72	81	90
10	0	10	20	30	40	50	60	70	80	90	100

Transparency Master

Name _____   Date _____

Small Multiplication Tables

×	0	1	2	3	4	5	6	7	8	9	10
0	0	0	0	0	0	0	0	0	0	0	0
1	0	1	2	3	4	5	6	7	8	9	10
2	0	2	4	6	8	10	12	14	16	18	20
3	0	3	6	9	12	15	18	21	24	27	30
4	0	4	8	12	16	20	24	28	32	36	40
5	0	5	10	15	20	25	30	35	40	45	50
6	0	6	12	18	24	30	36	42	48	54	60
7	0	7	14	21	28	35	42	49	56	63	70
8	0	8	16	24	32	40	48	56	64	72	80
9	0	9	18	27	36	45	54	63	72	81	90
10	0	10	20	30	40	50	60	70	80	90	100

×	0	1	2	3	4	5	6	7	8	9	10
0	0	0	0	0	0	0	0	0	0	0	0
1	0	1	2	3	4	5	6	7	8	9	10
2	0	2	4	6	8	10	12	14	16	18	20
3	0	3	6	9	12	15	18	21	24	27	30
4	0	4	8	12	16	20	24	28	32	36	40
5	0	5	10	15	20	25	30	35	40	45	50
6	0	6	12	18	24	30	36	42	48	54	60
7	0	7	14	21	28	35	42	49	56	63	70
8	0	8	16	24	32	40	48	56	64	72	80
9	0	9	18	27	36	45	54	63	72	81	90
10	0	10	20	30	40	50	60	70	80	90	100

×	0	1	2	3	4	5	6	7	8	9	10
0	0	0	0	0	0	0	0	0	0	0	0
1	0	1	2	3	4	5	6	7	8	9	10
2	0	2	4	6	8	10	12	14	16	18	20
3	0	3	6	9	12	15	18	21	24	27	30
4	0	4	8	12	16	20	24	28	32	36	40
5	0	5	10	15	20	25	30	35	40	45	50
6	0	6	12	18	24	30	36	42	48	54	60
7	0	7	14	21	28	35	42	49	56	63	70
8	0	8	16	24	32	40	48	56	64	72	80
9	0	9	18	27	36	45	54	63	72	81	90
10	0	10	20	30	40	50	60	70	80	90	100

×	0	1	2	3	4	5	6	7	8	9	10
0	0	0	0	0	0	0	0	0	0	0	0
1	0	1	2	3	4	5	6	7	8	9	10
2	0	2	4	6	8	10	12	14	16	18	20
3	0	3	6	9	12	15	18	21	24	27	30
4	0	4	8	12	16	20	24	28	32	36	40
5	0	5	10	15	20	25	30	35	40	45	50
6	0	6	12	18	24	30	36	42	48	54	60
7	0	7	14	21	28	35	42	49	56	63	70
8	0	8	16	24	32	40	48	56	64	72	80
9	0	9	18	27	36	45	54	63	72	81	90
10	0	10	20	30	40	50	60	70	80	90	100

Completing the Table

You should have only 20 blank squares left in your multiplication table. Use any strategy you like—skip counting, a calculator, a number line, or counters—to find the remaining facts.

When you find a fact, such as 4 × 6, you can also record its turn-around fact—in this case, 6 × 4.

Patterns for Nine

1. Copy and complete the list of facts for 9. Then write the products in a column, one on each line.

   0 × 9 = ?

   1 × 9 = ?

   2 × 9 = ?

   3 × 9 = ?

   4 × 9 = ?

   5 × 9 = ?

   6 × 9 = ?

   7 × 9 = ?

   8 × 9 = ?

   9 × 9 = ?

2. What patterns do you see in your list?

Completing the Table   SG • Grade 3 • Unit 11 • Lesson 4   149

Student Guide - page 149

Student Guide (p. 149)

1. 0, 9, 18, 27, 36, 45, 54, 63, 72, 81
2. Answers will vary.*

3. Use your calculator to find the products below. Then add the digits in each product. Repeat adding the digits until you get a one digit number.

   Example: 9 × 634 = 5706   5 + 7 + 0 + 6 = 18   1 + 8 = 9

   A. 9 × 47   **B.** 9 × 83
   C. 9 × 89   **D.** 9 × 92
   E. 9 × 123   **F.** 9 × 633
   G. 9 × 697   **H.** 9 × 333

4. Describe what happens when you add the digits of a multiple of 9.

Multiplication Facts and Triangle Flash Cards

Practice multiplication facts with a partner. Use your *Triangle Flash Cards: 5s* and *Triangle Flash Cards: 10s,* and follow the directions below.

- One partner covers the shaded number, the largest number on the card. This number will be the answer to the multiplication problem. It is called the **product.**

   5 × 4 = ?

   4 × 5 = ?

- The second person multiplies the two uncovered numbers (one in a circle, one in a square). These are the two **factors.** It doesn't matter which of the factors is said first. 4 × 5 and 5 × 4 both equal 20.

- Divide the cards into three piles: those facts you know and can answer quickly, those you can figure out with a strategy, and those you need to learn.

150   SG • Grade 3 • Unit 11 • Lesson 4   Completing the Table

Student Guide - page 150

Student Guide (p. 150)

3. **A.** 423; $4 + 2 + 3 = 9$*

   B. 747; $7 + 4 + 7 = 18$*

   C. 801; $8 + 0 + 1 = 9$

   D. 828; $8 + 2 + 8 = 18$

   E. 1107; $1 + 1 + 0 + 7 = 9$

   F. 5697; $5 + 6 + 9 + 7 = 27$

   G. 6273; $6 + 2 + 7 + 3 = 18$

   H. 2997; $2 + 9 + 9 + 7 = 27$

4. The sum is a multiple of 9.

*Answers and/or discussion are included in the Lesson Guide.

Student Guide (p. 151)

Homework

1. 12		**2.** 42	
3. 30		**4.** 20	
5. 63		**6.** 8	
7. 40		**8.** 64	
9. 28		**10.** 0	
11. 21		**12.** 54	
13. 48		**14.** 56	
15. 81		**16.** 35	
17. 54		**18.** 24	
19. 24		**20.** 24	
21. 9		**22.** 32	
23. 36		**24.** 49	

25. Answers will vary.

Student Guide - page 151

Discovery Assignment Book (p. 156)

Home Practice*

Part 1

1. 90

2. 70

3. 80

4. 18

5. 47

6. 56

7. A. $1.75

B. Answers will vary. Examples: 7 quarters or 1 quarter, 5 dimes, and 20 nickels

Part 2

1. 1300

2. 1200

3. 1400

4. 550

5. 657

6. A. 189 students

B. 495 students

Discovery Assignment Book - page 156

*Answers for all the Home Practice in the *Discovery Assignment Book* are at the end of the unit.

Lesson 5

Floor Tiler

Lesson Overview

Estimated Class Sessions

1

After spinning two numbers, a player uses their product to color in grid squares in the shape of a rectangle on his or her grid paper. Players take turns spinning and filling in their grids.

Key Content

- Practicing multiplication facts.
- Using the array model of multiplication to learn the multiplication facts.

Math Facts

DPP Task N provides practice with multiplication facts.

Homework

Students play *Floor Tiler* at home.

Assessment

Use the *Observational Assessment Record* to note students' abilities to represent multiplication using rectangular arrays.

Materials List

Supplies and Copies

Student	Teacher
Supplies for Each Student • crayon or marker **Supplies for Each Student Pair** • clear plastic spinner or pencil and paper clip	**Supplies**
Copies • 1 copy of *Centimeter Grid Paper* per student (*Unit Resource Guide* Page 52)	**Copies/Transparencies** • 1 transparency of *Centimeter Grid Paper,* optional (*Unit Resource Guide* Page 52) • 1 transparency of *Spinners 1–4 and 1–10,* optional (*Discovery Assignment Book* Page 173)

All blackline masters including assessment, transparency, and DPP masters are also on the Teacher Resource CD.

Student Books
Floor Tiler (*Discovery Assignment Book* Pages 171–172)
Spinners 1–4 and 1–10 (*Discovery Assignment Book* Page 173)

Daily Practice and Problems and Home Practice
DPP items M–N (*Unit Resource Guide* Pages 21–22)

Note: Classrooms whose pacing differs significantly from the suggested pacing of the units should use the Math Facts Calendar in Section 4 of the *Facts Resource Guide* to ensure students receive the complete math facts program.

Assessment Tools
Observational Assessment Record (*Unit Resource Guide* Pages 13–14)

M. Bit: Missing Time (URG p. 21)

Copy each list below. Find the missing times.

1. 2:50, 2:55, ___, 3:05, ___, ___, 3:20

2. 4:15, 4:30, ___, ___, 5:15, ___, 5:45

3. 6:00, 5:55, ___, 5:45, ___, ___, 5:30, ___

4. 8:30, ___, 7:30, ___, 6:30, 6:00, ___

N. Task: Multiplication and Rectangles (URG p. 22)

A rectangle is made from 3 rows with 8 tiles in each row.

1. Draw this rectangle on *Centimeter Grid Paper*.

2. How many tiles make up the rectangle? Write a number sentence to show your answer.

3. Make a different rectangle with the same number of tiles. How many rows? How many tiles in each row?

Before the Activity

Each student will need one-half sheet of *Centimeter Grid Paper.* Ask pairs to cut the grid in half or have the sheets cut ahead of time.

Teaching the Game

This game is for 2–4 players. The rules for playing *Floor Tiler* are found on the *Floor Tiler* Game Pages in the *Discovery Assignment Book.* A student spins to find two numbers for a multiplication sentence. He or she may use either two spins from one spinner or one spin from each spinner. After finding the product, the player colors in a rectangle with that number of squares, outlining this rectangle and recording its number sentence inside. Players continue in this fashion until one player fills in his or her grid completely. You may want to demonstrate the game using a transparency of *Centimeter Grid Paper* while a volunteer spins the spinners.

A good strategy is to use two spins from *Spinner 1–10* at the beginning of the game and two spins from *Spinner 1–4* near the end of the game. This way, the player gets to fill in large rectangles when his or her grid is empty and small rectangles when space gets tight. Encourage students to try a variety of strategies.

It will become difficult to fill in the grid completely when only a few squares are left. Rule #8 deals with this situation. If no player is able to color in a rectangle in three rounds of spinning, the player with the fewest squares left is the winner. This rule is helpful if students find the end of the game too slow moving.

Discovery Assignment Book - page 171

Discovery Assignment Book - page 172

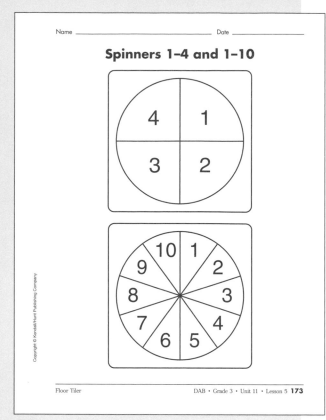

Name _____ Date _____

Spinners 1–4 and 1–10

Floor Tiler   DAB • Grade 3 • Unit 11 • Lesson 5 **173**

Discovery Assignment Book - page 173

Math Facts

DPP Task N provides practice with multiplication facts using rectangular arrays.

Homework and Practice

- Students can take home the Game Pages and grid paper and use pencil-and-paper-clip spinners to play at home. They record the number of minutes they play with family members or friends.

- DPP Bit M asks students to skip count to measure time by various intervals.

Assessment

Use the *Observational Assessment Record* to assess students' abilities to represent multiplication using rectangular arrays.

Extension

You can also play this game as a class by using transparencies of the spinners. Each student will fill in a rectangle on his or her half-sheet of *Centimeter Grid Paper.* Since players will fill in the grid differently, they will finish at different times. The first to finish is the winner.

Math Facts and Daily Practice and Problems

DPP Bit M provides practice with time and Task N provides practice with multiplication facts.

Teaching the Game

1. Students read the rules on the *Floor Tiler* Game Pages in the *Discovery Assignment Book.*
2. Students play *Floor Tiler* in groups of 2–4.

Homework

Students play *Floor Tiler* at home.

Assessment

Use the *Observational Assessment Record* to note students' abilities to represent multiplication using rectangular arrays.

Extension

Use transparencies of the spinners to play this game as a class.

Notes:

Lesson 6

Division in Lizardland

Lesson Overview

Estimated Class Sessions

1

Students explore the relationship between multiplication and division through problems about the Lizardland Amusement Park. They discover that there is no turn-around rule for division; they investigate division involving zero; and they look at the relationship between multiplication and division.

Key Content

- Solving problems involving division.
- Investigating division involving zero.
- Investigating whether there is a turn-around rule for division.
- Writing number sentences for division situations.

Math Facts

DPP items O and P provide practice with multiplication facts.

Homework

1. Assign the Homework section of the *Division in Lizardland* Activity Pages.
2. Assign Parts 3 and 4 of the Home Practice.

Assessment

Use *Question 17* of the Homework section as an assessment.

Curriculum Sequence

Before This Unit

Students explored concepts of division in Unit 7 Lesson 4 *Birthday Party* and Lesson 5 *The Money Jar.*

After This Unit

Students will revisit division in Unit 19.

Materials List

Supplies and Copies

Student	Teacher
Supplies for Each Student • counters, optional	**Supplies**
Copies • 1 completed copy of *My Multiplication Table* per student (*Discovery Assignment Book* Page 159)	**Copies/Transparencies** • 1 classroom copy of Lizardland poster from Lesson 1, optional

All blackline masters including assessment, transparency, and DPP masters are also on the Teacher Resource CD.

Student Books
Division in Lizardland (*Student Guide* Pages 152–154)

Daily Practice and Problems and Home Practice
DPP items O–P (*Unit Resource Guide* Pages 22–23)
Home Practice Parts 3–4 (*Discovery Assignment Book* Page 157)

Note: Classrooms whose pacing differs significantly from the suggested pacing of the units should use the Math Facts Calendar in Section 4 of the *Facts Resource Guide* to ensure students receive the complete math facts program.

Daily Practice and Problems

Suggestions for using the DPPs are on page 80.

O. Bit: Lizardland (URG p. 22)

Use the picture of Lizardland in the *Student Guide* to help you solve the following problems.

Find the Lizardland wall at the entrance to the park.

1. How many bricks are behind the Lizardland sign? Tell how you know.
2. How many bricks are covered by the sign listing the admission prices? Tell how you know.

P. Task: How Much and How Many? (URG p. 23)

A. Moe spent 9 nickels and 7 dimes to buy ice cream. How much money did he spend? Show how you found your answer.
B. Joe has 5 shirts. Each shirt has 3 pockets. How many pockets are on Joe's shirts? Write a number sentence.
C. Flo has 7 braids in her hair. Each braid has 5 beads. How many beads are in Flo's hair? Write a number sentence.

Students begin by completing *Questions 1–7* from *Division in Lizardland* Activity Pages in the *Student Guide*. To find the information needed to solve the problems, they refer to the picture of Lizardland in Lesson 1 of the *Student Guide*.

Each problem can be solved using division. Some students may use the related multiplication facts or repeated subtraction, and some students will need to model the problems with counters or pictures. Encourage students to use the multiplication facts they have been working with to obtain the related division facts. As students share how they found their answers, write number sentences on the board and discuss the relationship between multiplication and division. Point out that a problem such as 21 ÷ 7 can be solved by thinking:

- *How many 7s are there in 21?* or
- *What number times 7 equals 21?*

Multiplication facts and their related division facts are often referred to as **fact families.** Students might want to use their completed copy of *My Multiplication Table*.

Questions 4 and *5* provide an opportunity to discuss whether there is a turn-around rule for division. In *Question 4,* Mrs. Moore has three oranges to share among six people: $3 \div 6 = \frac{1}{2}$. Drawing a picture can help students solve this problem. In *Question 5,* Mrs. Moore shares six cookies among her three children: $6 \div 3 = 2$. Use these examples to point out that changing the order of the terms in a division sentence, unlike a multiplication sentence, does change the answer. *There is no turn-around rule for division.*

Questions 6 and *7* provide an opportunity to discuss division involving zero. In *Question 6,* Mr. Moore has zero cupcakes to share among six people. Each person receives zero cupcakes, so 0 ÷ 6 = 0. In fact, *0 divided by any non-zero number is 0.* In *Question 7,* the ticket taker has 100 game tokens to distribute to the families as they enter the park. Students examine what will happen if he distributes different numbers of tokens to the families. Depending on how many he gives to each family, he runs out after different numbers: Giving 4 game tokens to each family, he runs out after 25 families enter; giving 2 tokens, 50 families; giving 1 token, 100 families. These situations can be represented by these division sentences: 100 ÷ 4 = 25, 100 ÷ 2 = 50, and 100 ÷ 1 = 100. If, however, he gives 0 game tokens to each family as they enter, then more and more families will enter the park, but he will never run out of tokens. Therefore, there is no numerical value for

---

Division in Lizardland

Look at the picture of Lizardland to help you solve the following problems. Write number sentences to show the answers.

The Brownies

1. There are 21 Brownies and 3 leaders near Picnic Park. To make sure no one gets lost, the leaders split the troop into three smaller groups; each has its own adult leader. Each group is the same size. How many Brownies are in each group?

2. The 21 Brownies and their 3 leaders rode the Leaping Lizard Roller Coaster. How many cars on the roller coaster did they fill?

3. Each table in Picnic Park can seat eight people. Are there enough empty tables for the Brownies and their leaders?

The Moore Family

4. The Moore family is having a picnic by Lizard Lake. Mrs. Moore brought three large oranges to be shared among her family of six. How much will each person get? Write a division sentence for your answer.

5. Mrs. Moore brought six cookies to be shared among her 3 children. How many cookies will each child get? Write a division sentence for your answer. Compare your number sentence with the one you got for Question 4.

Student Guide - page 152 (Answers on p. 83)

Zero

6. Mr. Moore baked some cupcakes for his family to share. Unfortunately, he didn't remember to bring them, so he had zero cupcakes to share among six people. Use this story to write about the value of 0 ÷ 6.

7. The ticket taker has 100 game tokens to give to the first several families who enter the park.

   A. If he gives 4 game tokens to each family that enters the park, how many families will get four tokens before he runs out? If he gives 2 game tokens to each family, how many families will get before he runs out? How many families will get a token if he gives 1 token to each family? Be sure to write number sentences to show your answers.

   B. If he gives 0 tokens to each family, how many families will enter the park before he runs out of tokens? Use this story to tell about the value of 100 ÷ 0.

Fact Families

Multiplication and division facts are related. Questions 8–10 will show you what they have in common. The four facts in each question make up a **fact family.**

8.	A. 4 × 5 = ?	9.	A. 2 × 9 = ?	10.	A. 6 × 8 = ?
	B. 5 × 4 = ?		B. 9 × 2 = ?		B. 8 × 6 = ?
	C. 20 ÷ 5 = ?		C. 18 ÷ 2 = ?		C. 48 ÷ 8 = ?
	D. 20 ÷ 4 = ?		D. 18 ÷ 9 = ?		D. 48 ÷ 6 = ?

Division Symbols

The symbols in these division sentences mean the same thing:

$$24 \div 6 = 4 \qquad 24/6 = 4 \qquad 6\overline{)24}^{\,4}$$

11. 16/4 = ?   12. 45 ÷ 9 = ?

13. $\dfrac{?}{8\overline{)64}}$ 14. $\dfrac{?}{5\overline{)40}}$

Student Guide - page 153 (Answers on p. 83)

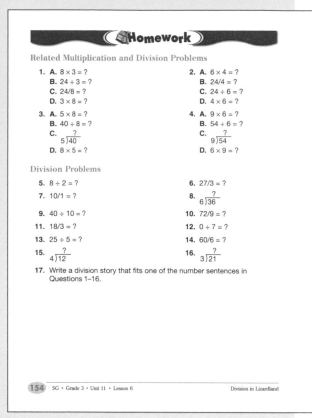

Student Guide - page 154 *(Answers on p. 84)*

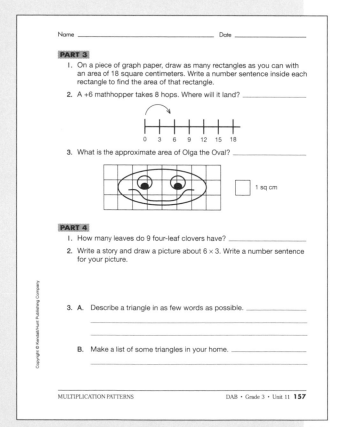

Discovery Assignment Book - page 157 *(Answers on p. 84)*

100 ÷ 0. We say that *division by 0 is undefined.* (See the Background for a discussion of division by zero.)

Questions 8–10 show students number sentences for related fact families. These problems can be done aloud as a group, individually on paper, or with a partner.

Questions 11–14 are division problems similar to those in the homework problems. Point out to students that they will see three different symbols for division: $24 \div 6$, $\frac{24}{6}$, and $6\overline{)24}$. As you write division sentences on the board, vary the notation so students will become familiar with all three.

Math Facts

DPP Bit O practices multiplication facts using rectangular arrays in the Lizardland picture. Task P provides practice with the multiplication facts for the 5s and 10s in word problems.

Homework and Practice

- Assign the problems in the Homework section of the *Division in Lizardland* Activity Pages in the *Student Guide.* Have students take home completed multiplication tables for this work.

- Parts 3 and 4 of the Home Practice can be assigned for homework.

Answers for Parts 3 and 4 of the Home Practice are in the Answer Key at the end of this lesson and at the end of this unit.

Assessment

Students can write an answer for homework *Question 17* in class as an assessment of their understanding of division.

Literature Connection

At this point, students will have learned that, unlike the commutative multiplication sentences, order is very important in division sentences. They might enjoy hearing the following excerpt from *Alice in Wonderland**, in which the Mad Hatter points out several other places where order is important.

> The Hatter opened his eyes very wide on hearing this; but all he *said* was, "Why is a raven like a writing-desk?"

> "Come, we shall have some fun now!" thought Alice. "I'm glad they've begun asking riddles—I believe I can guess that," she added aloud.

> "Do you mean that you think you can find out the answer to it?" said the March Hare.

> "Exactly so," said Alice.

> "Then you should say what you mean," the March Hare went on.

> "I do," Alice hastily replied; "at least—at least I mean what I say—that's the same thing, you know."

> "Not the same thing a bit!" said the Hatter. "Why, you might just as well say that 'I see what I eat' is the same thing as 'I eat what I see!'"

> "You might just as well say," added the March Hare, "that 'I like what I get' is the same thing as 'I get what I like!'"

> "You might just as well say," added the Dormouse, which seemed to be talking in its sleep, "that 'I breathe when I sleep' is the same thing as 'I sleep when I breathe!'"

> "It *is* the same thing with you," said the Hatter, and here the conversation dropped, and the party sat silent for a minute, while Alice thought over all she could remember about ravens and writing-desks, which wasn't much.

*Carroll, Lewis. *Alice's Adventures in Wonderland.* Illustrated by Helen Oxenbury. 1st Candlewick Press Edition. Candlewick Press, Cambridge, MA, 1999.

At a Glance

Math Facts and Daily Practice and Problems

DPP items O and P provide practice with multiplication facts.

Teaching the Activity

1. Students complete *Questions 1–5* from the *Division in Lizardland* Activity Pages in the *Student Guide* using the Lizardland picture as a reference.
2. Students share how they solved each problem and compare number sentences to look at the relationship between multiplication and division.
3. Students complete *Questions 6–7* and discuss division involving zero.
4. Students complete *Questions 8–10* on fact families.
5. Students complete *Questions 11–14* using three different symbols for division.

Homework

1. Assign the Homework section of the *Division in Lizardland* Activity Pages.
2. Assign Parts 3 and 4 of the Home Practice.

Assessment

Use *Question 17* of the Homework section as an assessment.

Connection

Read and discuss commutativity in an excerpt from *Alice in Wonderland*.

Answer Key is on pages 83–84.

Notes:

Student Guide (p. 152)

Division in Lizardland

Number sentences will vary.*

1. 7 Brownies; $21 \div 3 = 7$ Brownies
2. 6 cars; $24 \div 4 = 6$ cars
3. Yes; $8 \times 3 = 24$
4. $\frac{1}{2}$ orange; $3 \div 6 = \frac{1}{2}$ orange*
5. 2 cookies; $6 \div 3 = 2$ cookies*

Division in Lizardland

Look at the picture of Lizardland to help you solve the following problems. Write number sentences to show the answers.

The Brownies

1. There are 21 Brownies and 3 leaders near Picnic Park. To make sure no one gets lost, the leaders split the troop into three smaller groups; each has its own adult leader. Each group is the same size. How many Brownies are in each group?

2. The 21 Brownies and their 3 leaders rode the Leaping Lizard Roller Coaster. How many cars on the roller coaster did they fill?

3. Each table in Picnic Park can seat eight people. Are there enough empty tables for the Brownies and their leaders?

The Moore Family

4. The Moore family is having a picnic by Lizard Lake. Mrs. Moore brought three large oranges to be shared among her family of six. How much will each person get? Write a division sentence for your answer.

5. Mrs. Moore brought six cookies to be shared among her 3 children. How many cookies will each child get? Write a division sentence for your answer. Compare your number sentence with the one you got for Question 4.

152 SG • Grade 3 • Unit 11 • Lesson 6   Division in Lizardland

Student Guide - page 152

Student Guide (p. 153)

6. Since there are no cupcakes, each person will get 0 cupcakes.*

7. **A.** $100 \div 4 = 25$ families;
   $100 \div 2 = 50$ families;
   $100 \div 1 = 100$ families*

   B. No answer; he will never run out of tokens. An endless amount of people could enter and he would still have the 100 tokens. So $100 \div 0$ does not make sense (it is not defined).

8. **A.** 20   **B.** 20   **C.** 4   **D.** 5
9. **A.** 18   **B.** 18   **C.** 9   **D.** 2
10. **A.** 48   **B.** 48   **C.** 6   **D.** 8
11. 4
12. 5
13. 8
14. 2

Zero

6. Mr. Moore baked some cupcakes for his family to share. Unfortunately, he didn't remember to bring them, so he had zero cupcakes to share among six people. Use this story to write about the value of $0 \div 6$.

7. The ticket taker has 100 game tokens to give to the first several families who enter the park.

   A. If he gives 4 game tokens to each family that enters the park, how many families will get four tokens before he runs out? If he gives 2 game tokens to each family, how many families will enter before he runs out? How many families will get a token if he gives 1 token to each family? Be sure to write number sentences to show your answers.

   B. If he gives 0 tokens to each family, how many families will enter the park before he runs out of tokens? Use this story to tell about the value of $100 \div 0$.

Fact Families

Multiplication and division facts are related. Questions 8–10 will show you what they have in common. The four facts in each question make up a **fact family**.

8. **A.** $4 \times 5 = ?$ 9. **A.** $2 \times 9 = ?$ 10. **A.** $6 \times 8 = ?$
   B. $5 \times 4 = ?$ **B.** $9 \times 2 = ?$ **B.** $8 \times 6 = ?$
   C. $20 \div 5 = ?$ **C.** $18 \div 2 = ?$ **C.** $48 \div 8 = ?$
   D. $20 \div 4 = ?$ **D.** $18 \div 9 = ?$ **D.** $48 \div 6 = ?$

Division Symbols

The symbols in these division sentences mean the same thing:

$24 \div 6 = 4$ $24/6 = 4$ $6\overline{)24}^{\,4}$

11. $16/4 = ?$ 12. $45 \div 9 = ?$

13. $8\overline{)64}^{\,?}$ 14. $5\overline{)40}^{\,?}$

Division in Lizardland   SG • Grade 3 • Unit 11 • Lesson 6   153

Student Guide - page 153

*Answers and/or discussion are included in the Lesson Guide.

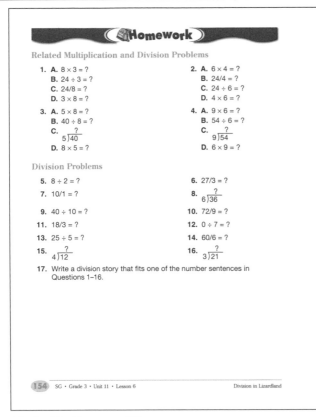

Student Guide - page 154

Student Guide (p. 154)

Homework

1. A. 24
    B. 8
    C. 3
    D. 24

2. A. 24
    B. 6
    C. 4
    D. 24

3. A. 40
    B. 5
    C. 8
    D. 40

4. A. 54
    B. 9
    C. 6
    D. 54

5. 4
6. 9
7. 10
8. 6
9. 4
10. 8
11. 6
12. 0
13. 5
14. 10
15. 3
16. 7
17. Answers will vary.

Discovery Assignment Book (p. 157)

Home Practice*

Part 3

1. Combinations for rectangle dimensions:
    1 cm by 18 cm rectangle or 18 cm by 1 cm;
    2 cm by 9 cm rectangle or 9 cm by 2 cm;
    3 cm by 6 cm rectangle or 6 cm by 3 cm
    rectangle

2. 48

3. 10–12 sq cm

Part 4

1. 36 leaves

2. Answers will vary. $6 \times 3 = 18$.

3. A. Answers will vary. A 3-sided closed figure
    with 3 angles. The 3 sides come together at
    3 corners.

    B. Answers will vary.

Discovery Assignment Book - page 157

*Answers for all the Home Practice in the *Discovery Assignment Book* are at the end of the unit.

Lesson 7

Cipher Force!

Lesson Overview

Estimated Class Sessions **1**

The Cipher Force is a team of four superheroes and their sidekick. The superheroes—Multiply by Zero, Divide by Zero, Add Zero, and Subtract Zero—embody basic operations with zero. Several silly adventures show what happens when you use these operations with zero.

Key Content

- Identifying and using patterns in addition, subtraction, and multiplication with zero.
- Understanding why division by zero is impossible.

Key Vocabulary

- cipher
- null

Math Facts

DPP Bit Q provides practice with multiplication facts using mathhoppers. Task R examines products of 36.

Homework

Remind students to practice at home for the quiz on the multiplication facts using the *Triangle Flash Cards: 5s* and *10s*.

Assessment

1. To assess this lesson, students can write a response to one of the first three Journal Prompts.
2. Use DPP item R to assess students' abilities to write number sentences for multiplication situations.

Materials List

Supplies and Copies

Student	Teacher
Supplies for Each Student	**Supplies**
Copies	**Copies/Transparencies**

All blackline masters including assessment, transparency, and DPP masters are also on the Teacher Resource CD.

Student Books

Cipher Force! (*Adventure Book* Pages 77–94)

Daily Practice and Problems and Home Practice

DPP items Q–R (*Unit Resource Guide* Pages 23–24)

Note: Classrooms whose pacing differs significantly from the suggested pacing of the units should use the Math Facts Calendar in Section 4 of the *Facts Resource Guide* to ensure students receive the complete math facts program.

Daily Practice and Problems

Suggestions for using the DPPs are on page 93.

Q. Bit: Mathhoppers (URG p. 23)

1. A +3 mathhopper starts at 0 and hops six times. Where does it land?
2. A +5 mathhopper starts at 0 and hops eight times. Where does it land?
3. A +5 mathhopper starts at 0 and wants to eat a sunflower seed on 163. Will it be able to land on the sunflower seed? Why or why not? Think about the patterns you found in your multiplication table.

R. Task: A Product of 36
(URG p. 24)

Write 36 as a product of two numbers in as many ways as you can.

In the story, the superhero Divide by Zero attempts to carry out two divisions by zero. Once, he designs a roller coaster with room for zero passengers in each car; another time, he invents a 0 Mathhopper. To make these episodes more accessible, discuss similar problems that do not involve zero before you read the story. For example, ask:

- *How many roller coaster cars are required for 24 Girl Scouts if each car can carry 4 girls?*

Link this problem with the number sentence $24 \div 4 = N$ and with a solution using repeated subtraction. The story puts 24 Girl Scouts on a silly roller coaster where each car carries 0 girls. This is linked to the number sentence $24 \div 0 = N$. It is "solved" using repeated subtraction.

You can also discuss how many hops various Mathhoppers need to hop to get from 0 to 100. The number sentence $100 \div 5 = N$ can be linked to the question:

- *How many hops does a +5 Mathhopper need to travel from 0 to 100?*

The story asks how many hops it would take a +0 Mathhopper to travel from 0 to 100. The number sentence that represents this question is $100 \div 0 = N$. See the Background in this unit for a further discussion of division by zero.

TIMS Tip

You may want to read the story twice: once to clarify the plot and again to draw out more of the mathematics.

Adventure Book - page 78

Page 78

- *What does* cipher *mean?*

Our word **cipher** comes from the Arabic word *sifr* meaning empty (as in an empty column on a counting board or abacus). *Zero* comes from the same root. Many mathematical terms derive from the Arabic language (e.g., *algebra, algorithm*) because of the work of medieval Arabic mathematicians.

- *Why is the Cipher Force's hideout called Null House?*

Null is another word for zero.

Adventure Book - page 79

Page 79

- *What does the Cipher Force insignia (⌀) stand for?*

The empty set; nothing.

Page 80

- *How would you explain to Mult why any number times zero is zero?*

One possibility: No matter how many sets or groups of zero you have, you still have zero.

Adventure Book - page 80

Page 81

- *What's wrong with Div's "zero coaster" idea?*

There is no true answer—he would never have enough cars.

- *What does Div's design have to do with dividing by zero?*

Division can be accomplished by repeatedly subtracting the divisor to make groups. See the Background for further discussion.

- *Show how Conrad could use his method to find how many baskets on a Ferris Wheel are needed if 15 people want to ride and each basket holds 3 people. What number sentence could go with this situation?*

$15 - 3 - 3 - 3 - 3 - 3 = 0$. Three was subtracted five times, so five baskets are needed. $15 \div 3 = 5$. Try more problems with different divisors and dividends; link each problem situation to a division sentence.

Adventure Book - page 81

Adventure Book - page 82

Adventure Book - page 85

Page 82

- *Which of the two sets of kids look more alike, Multiply by Zero and Divide by Zero or Add Zero and Subtract Zero?*

Add Zero and Subtract Zero are identical twins.

- *Which hero is wearing a cape?*

Multiply by Zero is wearing a cape.

- *Why do you suppose Add Zero and Subtract Zero look so much alike?*

Because adding and subtracting by zero yield the same result: the original number.

Page 85

- *Add Zero and Subtract Zero say they are completely different. Is that true?*

No, not only do they look quite similar, but their properties—addition with zero and subtraction with zero—always yield the same results: the original number.

- *Who else took from the rich and gave to the poor?*

Robin Hood and Zorro.

- *What happens when Subtract Zero takes nothing from the rich?*

Nothing. The rich still have the same amount of money.

- *What does this have to do with subtracting zero?*

They have exactly what they had before—this is the effect of subtracting zero.

Page 87

- *What happens when Add Zero gives nothing to the poor?*

Nothing.

- *What does this have to do with adding zero?*

They have exactly what they had before—this is the effect of adding zero.

Adventure Book - page 87

Page 90

- *Is Conrad speaking real English?*

Yes and no. Some of these words are made up, and some have to do with space travel or computers.

- *How do you think Cipher Force will fight the aliens?*

Answers will vary. Ask students to think about what each character usually does.

Adventure Book - page 90

Adventure Book - page 91

Adventure Book - page 92

Page 91

- *What will happen when Subtract Zero takes nothing from the aliens?*

Nothing.

- *What is a number sentence that might go with this?*

Aliens − 0 = Aliens

Page 92

- *What will happen when Add Zero adds nothing to her forces?*

Nothing.

- *What is a number sentence that might go with this?*

Forces + 0 = Forces

- *What does Div mean when he says "I'll finish them off none by none"?*

We usually say one by one (meaning one at a time). He will divide by using repeated subtraction; he'll subtract zero at a time.

- *Who defeats the aliens? Why?*

Mult does because multiplying anything by zero results in nothing (zero). She made nothing out of the aliens.

Page 94

- *Write a division problem for Div's new Mathhopper. Can you solve your problem?*

Example: How many hops does it take a 0 Mathhopper to get to 24? There is no answer to such a problem; it will never reach 24.

Journal Prompt

- Write an adventure for Zero the Digit, the new member of the Cipher Force. Tell how Zero the Digit plays an important role in writing numbers.

- Write about what happens when (1) you add zero to any number, (2) you subtract zero from any number, (3) you multiply any number by zero, and (4) you divide any number by zero.

- Explain to Div why his 0 Mathhopper won't ever get to 100.

- Who is the strongest member of the Cipher Force? Explain why his or her powers are the best.

Math Facts

DPP Bit Q provides practice with multiplication facts using mathhoppers.

Homework and Practice

Remind students to use the *Triangle Flash Cards: 5s* and *10s* to practice at home for the quiz on the multiplication facts.

Assessment

- To assess this lesson, students can write a response to one of the first three Journal Prompts.

- Use DPP item R to assess students' abilities to write number sentences for multiplication situations.

Adventure Book - page 94

Lesson 8

Multiples of Tens and Hundreds

Lesson Overview

Estimated Class Sessions
1-2

Using base-ten pieces, students investigate multiplication by multiples of 10 and 100.

Key Content

- Multiplying by tens and hundreds.
- Communicating patterns found when multiplying by tens and hundreds.

Math Facts

DPP Bit S is the Quiz on 5s and 10s. Task T builds number sense and provides practice with math facts.

Homework

Assign the *Professor Peabody's Multiplication Tables* Homework Page in the *Discovery Assignment Book*.

Assessment

1. Use DPP Bit S and the *Observational Assessment Record* to note students' fluency with the multiplication facts for the fives and tens.
2. Transfer appropriate documentation from the Unit 11 *Observational Assessment Record* to students' *Individual Assessment Record Sheets*.

Materials List

Supplies and Copies

Student	Teacher
Supplies for Each Student • calculator • set of base-ten pieces	**Supplies** • overhead base-ten pieces, optional
Copies • 1 completed copy of *My Multiplication Table* per student (*Discovery Assignment Book* Page 159)	**Copies/Transparencies** • 1 transparency of *Professor Peabody's Multiplication Tables* (*Discovery Assignment Book* Page 175)

All blackline masters including assessment, transparency, and DPP masters are also on the Teacher Resource CD.

Student Books

Multiples of Tens and Hundreds (*Student Guide* Page 155)
Professor Peabody's Multiplication Tables (*Discovery Assignment Book* Page 175)

Daily Practice and Problems and Home Practice

DPP items S–T (*Unit Resource Guide* Pages 24–25)

Note: Classrooms whose pacing differs significantly from the suggested pacing of the units should use the Math Facts Calendar in Section 4 of the *Facts Resource Guide* to ensure students receive the complete math facts program.

Assessment Tools

Observational Assessment Record (*Unit Resource Guide* Pages 13–14)
Individual Assessment Record Sheet (*Teacher Implementation Guide,* Assessment section)

Daily Practice and Problems

Suggestions for using the DPPs are on page 98.

S. Bit: Quiz on 5s and 10s (URG p. 24)

A. $5 \times 2 =$ B. $3 \times 10 =$

C. $5 \times 0 =$ D. $8 \times 10 =$

E. $6 \times 10 =$ F. $5 \times 3 =$

G. $10 \times 9 =$ H. $7 \times 5 =$

I. $10 \times 2 =$ J. $10 \times 7 =$

K. $6 \times 5 =$ L. $5 \times 10 =$

M. $8 \times 5 =$ N. $9 \times 5 =$

O. $4 \times 10 =$ P. $4 \times 5 =$

Q. $10 \times 10 =$ R. $5 \times 5 =$

T. Task: Mathhopper (URG p. 25)

You may use a calculator to solve the problems.
A +8 mathhopper starts at 0.

1. There is a frog at 97. Will the mathhopper land on the frog and be eaten? Tell how you know. If it does not land on the frog, how close does it get?

2. How many hops does the mathhopper need to take to get to a daisy at 224? Tell how you know.

In *Question 1* on the *Multiples of Tens and Hundreds* Activity Page in the *Student Guide,* students recall the pattern they found in their multiplication tables for multiplying a number by ten: Write a zero at the end of the number. In *Question 2,* they use this pattern to predict the result of multiplying two- and three-digit numbers by ten. Then they use their calculators to verify that the pattern of attaching a zero still holds.

Journal Prompt

Describe patterns for multiplying a number by 10, by 100, and by multiples of 10 and 100.

Questions 3–4 involve multiplying by tens and hundreds. Work together on an example of this type before students work on their own. Write "3 × 50" on the board and ask students to tell you the product and to describe how they solved the problem. Some might use repeated addition, and some might use the related fact 3 × 5 = 15. Model the problem using base-ten pieces, as shown in Figure 7. Show three groups of five skinnies. Students can count skinnies by tens to find that 3 × 50 = 150. Encourage them to use the base-ten pieces to solve the remaining problems.

$$3 \times 50 = 3 \times 5 \text{ tens}$$
$$= 15 \text{ tens}$$
$$\text{So, } 3 \times 50 = 150$$

Figure 7: *Modeling 3 × 50 with base-ten pieces*

Multiples of Tens and Hundreds

1. What pattern for multiplying a number by ten did you find in the multiplication table? Write two examples that show your pattern.

2. Use the pattern to predict these products. Use a calculator to check your predictions.
   A. 10 × 24 = ?   B. 10 × 37 = ?
   C. 10 × 40 = ?   D. 10 × 348 = ?
   E. 100 × 6 = ?   F. 100 × 12 = ?
   G. 100 × 34 = ?   H. 100 × 876 = ?

3. Solve the following problems.
   A. 2 × 3 = ?   B. 2 × 30 = ?   C. 2 × 300 = ?
   D. 2 × 4 = ?   E. 2 × 40 = ?   F. 2 × 400 = ?
   G. 3 × 6 = ?   H. 3 × 60 = ?   I. 3 × 600 = ?
   J. 4 × 3 = ?   K. 4 × 30 = ?   L. 4 × 300 = ?

4. Solve the following problems.

   A. 200   B. 300   C. 600
      ×5   ×3   ×4

   D. 500   E. 900   F. 600
      ×7   ×5   ×5

Student Guide **- page 155 (Answers on p. 100)**

Professor Peabody's
Multiplication Tables

Homework

Professor Peabody started to fill in the multiplication table below. He wanted to look for patterns. As he was working, a rare spotted mathhopper hopped by his window. He quickly picked up his net and followed it out the window.

Help Professor Peabody with his work by finishing this table for him. Look for patterns. On a separate sheet of paper, write a report that tells Professor Peabody about the patterns you find.

X	10	20	30	40	50	60	70	80	90	100
1									90	100
2			60					160	180	
3							210	240		
4						240	280			
5					250	300				500
6				240	300					
7			210	280						
8		160	240						720	
9	90	180								
10	100									

Copyright © Kendall/Hunt Publishing Company

Multiples of Tens and Hundreds   DAB • Grade 3 • Unit 11 • Lesson 8 **175**

Discovery Assignment Book - page 175 *(Answers on p. 100)*

Math Facts

DPP Task T uses mathhopper questions to build number sense and fluency with multiplication facts.

Homework and Practice

More practice with multiplying by tens is provided on the *Professor Peabody's Multiplication Tables* Homework Page in the *Discovery Assignment Book.*

Assessment

• DPP Bit S is a quiz on the 5s and 10s and assesses multiplication facts. Use the *Observational Assessment Record* to note students' fluency with the multiplication facts for the fives and tens.

• Transfer appropriate documentation from the Unit 11 *Observational Assessment Record* to students' *Individual Assessment Record Sheets.*

At a Glance

Math Facts and Daily Practice and Problems

DPP Bit S is the quiz on 5s and 10s. Task T builds number sense and practices math facts.

Teaching the Activity

Students complete *Questions 1–4* on the *Multiples of Tens and Hundreds* Activity Page in the *Student Guide*.

Homework

Assign the *Professor Peabody's Multiplication Table* Homework Page in the *Discovery Assignment Book*.

Assessment

1. Use DPP Bit S and the *Observational Assessment Record* to note students' fluency with the multiplication facts for the fives and tens.
2. Transfer appropriate documentation from the Unit 11 *Observational Assessment Record* to students' *Individual Assessment Record Sheets*.

Answer Key is on page 100.

Notes:

Student Guide (p. 155)

Multiples of Tens and Hundreds*

1. Put a 0 to the right of the number that is being multiplied by 10. For example, $4 \times 10 = 4\underline{0}$

2. **A.** 240   **B.** 370
    C. 400   **D.** 3480
    E. 600   **F.** 1200
    G. 3400   **H.** 87,600

3. **A.** 6   **B.** 60
    C. 600   **D.** 8
    E. 80   **F.** 800
    G. 18   **H.** 180
    I. 1800   **J.** 12
    K. 120   **L.** 1200

4. **A.** 1000   **B.** 900
    C. 2400   **D.** 3500
    E. 4500   **F.** 3000

Multiples of Tens and Hundreds

1. What pattern for multiplying a number by ten did you find in the multiplication table? Write two examples that show your pattern.

2. Use the pattern to predict these products. Use a calculator to check your predictions.
 A. $10 \times 24 = ?$ **B.** $10 \times 37 = ?$
 C. $10 \times 40 = ?$ **D.** $10 \times 348 = ?$
 E. $100 \times 6 = ?$ **F.** $100 \times 12 = ?$
 G. $100 \times 34 = ?$ **H.** $100 \times 876 = ?$

3. Solve the following problems.
 A. $2 \times 3 = ?$ **B.** $2 \times 30 = ?$ **C.** $2 \times 300 = ?$
 D. $2 \times 4 = ?$ **E.** $2 \times 40 = ?$ **F.** $2 \times 400 = ?$
 G. $3 \times 6 = ?$ **H.** $3 \times 60 = ?$ **I.** $3 \times 600 = ?$
 J. $4 \times 3 = ?$ **K.** $4 \times 30 = ?$ **L.** $4 \times 300 = ?$

4. Solve the following problems.
 A. $\begin{array}{r} 200 \\ \times 5 \\ \hline \end{array}$ **B.** $\begin{array}{r} 300 \\ \times 3 \\ \hline \end{array}$ **C.** $\begin{array}{r} 600 \\ \times 4 \\ \hline \end{array}$

 D. $\begin{array}{r} 500 \\ \times 7 \\ \hline \end{array}$ **E.** $\begin{array}{r} 900 \\ \times 5 \\ \hline \end{array}$ **F.** $\begin{array}{r} 600 \\ \times 5 \\ \hline \end{array}$

Multiples of Tens and Hundreds   SG • Grade 3 • Unit 11 • Lesson 8   **155**

Student Guide - page 155

Discovery Assignment Book (p. 175)

Professor Peabody's Multiplication Tables

×	10	20	30	40	50	60	70	80	90	100
1	10	20	30	40	50	60	70	80	90	100
2	20	40	60	80	100	120	140	160	180	200
3	30	60	90	120	150	180	210	240	270	300
4	40	80	120	160	200	240	280	320	360	400
5	50	100	150	200	250	300	350	400	450	500
6	60	120	180	240	300	360	420	480	540	600
7	70	140	210	280	350	420	490	560	630	700
8	80	160	240	320	400	480	560	640	720	800
9	90	180	270	360	450	540	630	720	810	900
10	100	200	300	400	500	600	700	800	900	1000

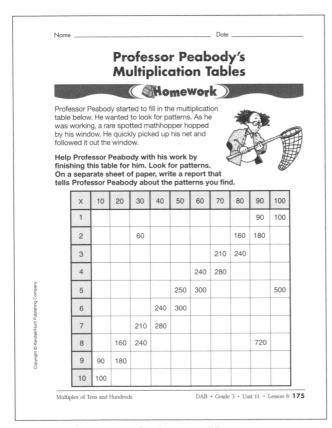

Name _____ Date _____

Professor Peabody's Multiplication Tables

Homework

Professor Peabody started to fill in the multiplication table below. He wanted to look for patterns. As he was working, a rare spotted mathhopper hopped by his window. He quickly picked up his net and followed it out the window.

Help Professor Peabody with his work by finishing this table for him. Look for patterns. On a separate sheet of paper, write a report that tells Professor Peabody about the patterns you find.

X	10	20	30	40	50	60	70	80	90	100
1									90	100
2			60					160	180	
3						210	240			
4					240	280				
5				250	300				500	
6			240	300						
7			210	280						
8		160	240					720		
9	90	180								
10	100									

Multiples of Tens and Hundreds   DAB • Grade 3 • Unit 11 • Lesson 8   **175**

Discovery Assignment Book - page 175

*Answers and/or discussion are included in the Lesson Guide.

Discovery Assignment Book (p. 156)

Home Practice

Part 1

I. 90	2. 70
3. 80	4. 18
5. 47	6. 56

7. **A.** $1.75

   B. Answers will vary. Examples: 7 quarters or 1 quarter, 5 dimes, and 20 nickels

Part 2

I. 1300	2. 1200
3. 1400	4. 550

5. 657

6. **A.** 189 students

   B. 495 students

Discovery Assignment Book - page 156

Discovery Assignment Book (p. 157)

Part 3

I. Combinations for rectangle dimensions:
   1 cm by 18 cm rectangle or 18 cm by 1 cm;
   2 cm by 9 cm rectangle or 9 cm by 2 cm;
   3 cm by 6 cm rectangle or 6 cm by 3 cm rectangle

2. 48

3. 10–12 sq cm

Part 4

I. 36 leaves

2. Answers will vary. $6 \times 3 = 18$.

3. **A.** Answers will vary. A 3-sided closed figure with 3 angles. The 3 sides come together at 3 corners.

   B. Answers will vary.

Discovery Assignment Book - page 157

*Answers and/or discussion are included in the Lesson Guide.

Glossary

This glossary provides definitions of key vocabulary terms in the Grade 3 lessons. Locations of key vocabulary terms in the curriculum are included with each definition. Components Key: URG = *Unit Resource Guide,* SG = *Student Guide,* and DAB = *Discovery Assignment Book.*

A

Area (URG Unit 5; SG Unit 5)
The area of a shape is the amount of space it covers, measured in square units.

Array (URG Unit 7 & Unit 11)
An array is an arrangement of elements into a rectangular pattern of (horizontal) rows and (vertical) columns. (*See* column and row.)

Associative Property of Addition (URG Unit 2)
For any three numbers a, b, and c we have $a + (b + c) = (a + b) + c$. For example in finding the sum of 4, 8, and 2, one can compute $4 + 8$ first and then add 2: $(4 + 8) + 2 = 14$. Alternatively, we can compute $8 + 2$ and then add the result to 4: $4 + (8 + 2) = 4 + 10 = 14$.

Average (URG Unit 5)
A number that can be used to represent a typical value in a set of data. (*See also* mean and median.)

Axes (URG Unit 8; SG Unit 8)
Reference lines on a graph. In the Cartesian coordinate system, the axes are two perpendicular lines that meet at the origin. The singular of axes is axis.

B

Base (of a cube model) (URG Unit 18; SG Unit 18)
The part of a cube model that sits on the "ground."

Base-Ten Board (URG Unit 4)
A tool to help children organize base-ten pieces when they are representing numbers.

Base-Ten Pieces (URG Unit 4; SG Unit 4)
A set of manipulatives used to model our number system as shown in the figure at the right. Note that a skinny is made of 10 bits, a flat is made of 100 bits, and a pack is made of 1000 bits.

Base-Ten Shorthand (SG Unit 4)
A pictorial representation of the base-ten pieces as shown.

Nickname	Picture	Shorthand
bit		·
skinny		/
flat		
pack		

Best-Fit Line (URG Unit 9; SG Unit 9; DAB Unit 9)
The line that comes closest to the most number of points on a point graph.

Bit (URG Unit 4; SG Unit 4)
A cube that measures 1 cm on each edge. It is the smallest of the base-ten pieces that is often used to represent 1. (*See also* base-ten pieces.)

C

Capacity (URG Unit 16)
1. The volume of the inside of a container.
2. The largest volume a container can hold.

Cartesian Coordinate System (URG Unit 8)
A method of locating points on a flat surface by means
of numbers. This method is named after its originator,
René Descartes. (*See also* coordinates.)

Centimeter (cm)
A unit of measure in the metric system equal to
one-hundredth of a meter. (1 inch = 2.54 cm)

Column (URG Unit 11)
In an array, the objects lined up vertically.

Common Fraction (URG Unit 15)
Any fraction that is written with a numerator and denom-
inator that are whole numbers. For example, $\frac{3}{4}$ and $\frac{9}{4}$ are
both common fractions. (*See also* decimal fraction.)

Commutative Property of Addition (URG Unit 2 &
    Unit 11)
This is also known as the Order Property of Addition.
Changing the order of the addends does not change the
sum. For example, $3 + 5 = 5 + 3 = 8$. Using variables,
$n + m = m + n$.

Commutative Property of Multiplication
    (URG Unit 11)
Changing the order of the factors in a multiplication
problem does not change the result, e.g.,
$7 \times 3 = 3 \times 7 = 21$. (*See also* turn-around facts.)

Congruent (URG Unit 12 & Unit 17; SG Unit 12)
Figures with the same shape and size.

Convenient Number (URG Unit 6)
A number used in computation that is close enough to
give a good estimate, but is also easy to compute men-
tally, e.g., 25 and 30 are convenient numbers for 27.

Coordinates (URG Unit 8; SG Unit 8)
An ordered pair of numbers that locates points on a flat
surface by giving distances from a pair of coordinate
axes. For example, if a point has coordinates (4, 5) it
is 4 units from the vertical axis and 5 units from the
horizontal axis.

Counting Back (URG Unit 2)
A strategy for subtracting in which students start from a
larger number and then count down until the number is
reached. For example, to solve $8 - 3$, begin with 8 and
count down three, 7, 6, 5.

Counting Down (*See* counting back.)

Counting Up (URG Unit 2)
A strategy for subtraction in which the student starts at
the lower number and counts on to the higher number.
For example, to solve $8 - 5$, the student starts at 5 and
counts up three numbers (6, 7, 8). So $8 - 5 = 3$.

Cube (SG Unit 18)
A three-dimensional shape with six congruent
square faces.

Cubic Centimeter (cc)
    (URG Unit 16; SG Unit 16)
The volume of a cube that is
one centimeter long on each edge.

cubic centimeter

Cup (URG Unit 16)
A unit of volume equal to
8 fluid ounces, one-half pint.

D

Decimal Fraction (URG Unit 15)
A fraction written as a decimal. For example, 0.75 and
0.4 are decimal fractions and $\frac{75}{100}$ and $\frac{4}{10}$ are called
common fractions. (*See also* fraction.)

Denominator (URG Unit 13)
The number below the line in a fraction. The denominator indicates the number of equal parts in which the unit
whole is divided. For example, the 5 is the denominator
in the fraction $\frac{2}{5}$. In this case the unit whole is divided into
five equal parts.

Density (URG Unit 16)
The ratio of an object's mass to its volume.

Difference (URG Unit 2)
The answer to a subtraction problem.

Dissection (URG Unit 12 & Unit 17)
Cutting or decomposing a geometric shape into smaller
shapes that cover it exactly.

Distributive Property of Multiplication over Addition
    (URG Unit 19)
For any three numbers *a, b,* and *c, a* $\times (b + c) =$
$a \times b + a \times c$. The distributive property is the foundation for most methods of multidigit multiplication. For
example, $9 \times (17) = 9 \times (10 + 7) = 9 \times 10 + 9 \times 7 =$
$90 + 63 = 153$.

E

Equal-Arm Balance
See two-pan balance.

Equilateral Triangle (URG Unit 7)
A triangle with all sides of equal length and all angles of equal measure.

Equivalent Fractions (SG Unit 17)
Fractions that have the same value, e.g., $\frac{2}{4} = \frac{1}{2}$.

Estimate (URG Unit 5 & Unit 6)
1. (verb) To find *about* how many.
2. (noun) An approximate number.

Extrapolation (URG Unit 7)
Using patterns in data to make predictions or to estimate values that lie beyond the range of values in the set of data.

F

Fact Family (URG Unit 11; SG Unit 11)
Related math facts, e.g., $3 \times 4 = 12$, $4 \times 3 = 12$, $12 \div 3 = 4$, $12 \div 4 = 3$.

Factor (URG Unit 11; SG Unit 11)
1. In a multiplication problem, the numbers that are multiplied together. In the problem $3 \times 4 = 12$, 3 and 4 are the factors.
2. Whole numbers that can be multiplied together to get a number. That is, numbers that divide a number evenly, e.g., 1, 2, 3, 4, 6, and 12 are all the factors of 12.

Fewest Pieces Rule (URG Unit 4 & Unit 6; SG Unit 4)
Using the least number of base-ten pieces to represent a number. (*See also* base-ten pieces.)

Flat (URG Unit 4; SG Unit 4)
A block that measures 1 cm × 10 cm × 10 cm. It is one of the base-ten pieces that is often used to represent 100. (*See also* base-ten pieces.)

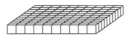

Flip (URG Unit 12)
A motion of the plane in which a figure is reflected over a line so that any point and its image are the same distance from the line.

Fraction (URG Unit 15)
A number that can be written as $\frac{a}{b}$ where a and b are whole numbers and b is not zero. For example, $\frac{1}{2}$, 0.5, and 2 are all fractions since 0.5 can be written as $\frac{5}{10}$ and 2 can be written as $\frac{2}{1}$.

Front-End Estimation (URG Unit 6)
Estimation by looking at the left-most digit.

G

Gallon (gal) (URG Unit 16)
A unit of volume equal to four quarts.

Gram
The basic unit used to measure mass.

H

Hexagon (SG Unit 12)
A six-sided polygon.

Horizontal Axis (SG Unit 1)
In a coordinate grid, the x-axis. The axis that extends from left to right.

I

Interpolation (URG Unit 7)
Making predictions or estimating values that lie between data points in a set of data.

J

K

Kilogram
1000 grams.

L

Likely Event (SG Unit 1)
An event that has a high probability of occurring.

Line of Symmetry (URG Unit 12)
A line is a line of symmetry for a plane figure if, when the figure is folded along this line, the two parts match exactly.

Line Symmetry (URG Unit 12; SG Unit 12)
A figure has line symmetry if it has at least one line of symmetry.

Liter (l) (URG Unit 16; SG Unit 16)
Metric unit used to measure volume. A liter is a little more than a quart.

M

Magic Square (URG Unit 2)
A square array of digits in which the sums of the rows, columns, and main diagonals are the same.

Making a Ten (URG Unit 2)
Strategies for addition and subtraction that make use of knowing the sums to ten. For example, knowing $6 + 4 = 10$ can be helpful in finding $10 - 6 = 4$ and $11 - 6 = 5$.

Mass (URG Unit 9 & Unit 16; SG Unit 9)
The amount of matter in an object.

Mean (URG Unit 5)
An average of a set of numbers that is found by adding the values of the data and dividing by the number of values.

Measurement Division (URG Unit 7)
Division as equal grouping. The total number of objects and the number of objects in each group are known. The number of groups is the unknown. For example, tulip bulbs come in packages of 8. If 216 bulbs are sold, how many packages are sold?

Measurement Error (URG Unit 9)
The unavoidable error that occurs due to the limitations inherent to any measurement instrument.

Median (URG Unit 5; DAB Unit 5)
For a set with an odd number of data arranged in order, it is the middle number. For an even number of data arranged in order, it is the number halfway between the two middle numbers.

Meniscus (URG Unit 16; SG Unit 16)
The curved surface formed when a liquid creeps up the side of a container (for example, a graduated cylinder).

Meter (m)
The standard unit of length measure in the metric system. One meter is approximately 39 inches.

Milliliter (ml) (URG Unit 16; SG Unit 16)
A measure of capacity in the metric system that is the volume of a cube that is one centimeter long on each edge.

Multiple (URG Unit 3 & Unit 11)
A number is a multiple of another number if it is evenly divisible by that number. For example, 12 is a multiple of 2 since 2 divides 12 evenly.

N

Numerator (URG Unit 13)
The number written above the line in a fraction. For example, the 2 is the numerator in the fraction $\frac{2}{5}$. (*See also* denominator.)

O

One-Dimensional Object (URG Unit 18; SG Unit 18)
An object is one-dimensional if it is made up of pieces of lines and curves.

Ordered Pairs (URG Unit 8)
A pair of numbers that gives the coordinates of a point on a grid in relation to the origin. The horizontal coordinate is given first; the vertical coordinate is given second. For example, the ordered pair (5, 3) tells us to move five units to the right of the origin and 3 units up.

Origin (URG Unit 8)
The point at which the *x*- and *y*-axes (horizontal and vertical axes) intersect on a coordinate plane. The origin is described by the ordered pair (0, 0) and serves as a reference point so that all the points on the plane can be located by ordered pairs.

P

Pack (URG Unit 4; SG Unit 4)
A cube that measures 10 cm on each edge. It is one of the base-ten pieces that is often used to represent 1000. (*See also* base-ten pieces.)

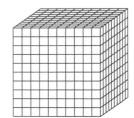

Palindrome (URG Unit 6)
A number, word, or phrase that reads the same forward and backward, e.g., 12321.

Parallel Lines (URG Unit 18)
Lines that are in the same direction. In the plane, parallel lines are lines that do not intersect.

Parallelogram (URG Unit 18)
A quadrilateral with two pairs of parallel sides.

Partitive Division (URG Unit 7)
Division as equal sharing. The total number of objects and the number of groups are known. The number of objects in each group is the unknown. For example, Frank has 144 marbles that he divides equally into 6 groups. How many marbles are in each group?

Pentagon (SG Unit 12)
A five-sided, five-angled polygon.

Perimeter (URG Unit 7; DAB Unit 7)
The distance around a two-dimensional shape.

Pint (URG Unit 16)
A unit of volume measure equal to 16 fluid ounces, i.e., two cups.

Polygon
A two-dimensional connected figure made of line segments in which each endpoint of every side meets with an endpoint of exactly one other side.

Population (URG Unit 1; SG Unit 1)
A collection of persons or things whose properties will be analyzed in a survey or experiment.

Prediction (SG Unit 1)
Using data to declare or foretell what is likely to occur.

Prime Number (URG Unit 11)
A number that has exactly two factors. For example, 7 has exactly two distinct factors, 1 and 7.

Prism
A three-dimensional figure that has two congruent faces, called bases, that are parallel to each other, and all other faces are parallelograms.

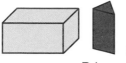

Prisms   Not a prism

Product (URG Unit 11; SG Unit 11; DAB Unit 11)
The answer to a multiplication problem. In the problem $3 \times 4 = 12$, 12 is the product.

Q

Quadrilateral (URG Unit 18)
A polygon with four sides.

Quart (URG Unit 16)
A unit of volume equal to 32 fluid ounces; one quarter of a gallon.

R

Recording Sheet (URG Unit 4)
A place value chart used for addition and subtraction problems.

Rectangular Prism (URG Unit 18; SG Unit 18)
A prism whose bases are rectangles. A right rectangular prism is a prism having all faces rectangles.

Regular (URG Unit 7; DAB Unit 7)
A polygon is regular if all sides are of equal length and all angles are equal.

Remainder (URG Unit 7)
Something that remains or is left after a division problem. The portion of the dividend that is not evenly divisible by the divisor, e.g., $16 \div 5 = 3$ with 1 as a remainder.

Right Angle (SG Unit 12)
An angle that measures 90°.

Rotation (turn) (URG Unit 12)
A transformation (motion) in which a figure is turned a specified angle and direction around a point.

Row (URG Unit 11)
In an array, the objects lined up horizontally.

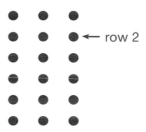

← row 2

Rubric (URG Unit 2)
A written guideline for assigning scores to student work, for the purpose of assessment.

S

Sample (URG Unit 1; SG Unit 1)
A part or subset of a population.

Skinny (URG Unit 4; SG Unit 4)
A block that measures 1 cm × 1 cm × 10 cm. It is one of the base-ten pieces that is often used to represent 10. (*See also* base-ten pieces.)

Square Centimeter (sq cm) (SG Unit 5)
The area of a square that is 1 cm long on each side.

Square Number (SG Unit 11)
A number that is the product of a whole number multiplied by itself. For example, 25 is a square number since $5 \times 5 = 25$. A square number can be represented by a square array with the same number of rows as columns. A square array for 25 has 5 rows of 5 objects in each row or 25 total objects.

Standard Masses
A set of objects with convenient masses, usually 1 g, 10 g, 100 g, etc.

Sum (URG Unit 2; SG Unit 2)
The answer to an addition problem.

Survey (URG Unit 14; SG Unit 14)
An investigation conducted by collecting data from a sample of a population and then analyzing it. Usually surveys are used to make predictions about the entire population.

T

Tangrams (SG Unit 12)
A type of geometric puzzle. A shape is given and it must be covered exactly with seven standard shapes called tans.

Thinking Addition (URG Unit 2)
A strategy for subtraction that uses a related addition problem. For example, $15 - 7 = 8$ because $8 + 7 = 15$.

Three-Dimensional (URG Unit 18; SG Unit 18)
Existing in three-dimensional space; having length, width, and depth.

TIMS Laboratory Method (URG Unit 1; SG Unit 1)
A method that students use to organize experiments and investigations. It involves four components: draw, collect, graph, and explore. It is a way to help students learn about the scientific method.

Turn (URG Unit 12)
(*See* rotation.)

Turn-Around Facts (URG Unit 2 & Unit 11 p. 37; SG Unit 11)
Addition facts that have the same addends but in a different order, e.g., $3 + 4 = 7$ and $4 + 3 = 7$. (*See also* commutative property of addition and commutative property of multiplication.)

Two-Dimensional (URG Unit 18; SG Unit 18)
Existing in the plane; having length and width.

Two-Pan Balance
A device for measuring the mass of an object by balancing the object against a number of standard masses (usually multiples of 1 unit, 10 units, and 100 units, etc.).

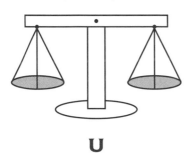

U

Unit (of measurement) (URG Unit 18)
A precisely fixed quantity used to measure. For example, centimeter, foot, kilogram, and quart are units of measurement.

Using a Ten (URG Unit 2)
1. A strategy for addition that uses partitions of the number 10. For example, one can find $8 + 6$ by thinking $8 + 6 = 8 + 2 + 4 = 10 + 4 = 14$.
2. A strategy for subtraction that uses facts that involve subtracting 10. For example, students can use $17 - 10 = 7$ to learn the "close fact" $17 - 9 = 8$.

Using Doubles (URG Unit 2)
Strategies for addition and subtraction that use knowing doubles. For example, one can find $7 + 8$ by thinking $7 + 8 = 7 + 7 + 1 = 14 + 1 = 15$. Knowing $7 + 7 = 14$ can be helpful in finding $14 - 7 = 7$ and $14 - 8 = 6$.

V

Value (URG Unit 1; SG Unit 1)
The possible outcomes of a variable. For example, red, green, and blue are possible values for the variable *color*. Two meters and 1.65 meters are possible values for the variable *length*.

Variable (URG Unit 1; SG Unit 1)
1. An attribute or quantity that changes or varies.
2. A symbol that can stand for a variable.

Vertex (URG Unit 12; SG Unit 12)
1. A point where the sides of a polygon meet.
2. A point where the edges of a three-dimensional object meet.

Vertical Axis (SG Unit 1)
In a coordinate grid, the *y*-axis. It is perpendicular to the horizontal axis.

Volume (URG Unit 16; SG Unit 16)
The measure of the amount of space occupied by an object.

Volume by Displacement (URG Unit 16)
A way of measuring volume of an object by measuring the amount of water (or some other fluid) it displaces.

W

Weight (URG Unit 9)
A measure of the pull of gravity on an object. One unit for measuring weight is the pound.

X

Y

Z